The Reminders

A Simple Buddhist Guide
to Living and Dying
Without Regret

Dennis Hunter

Copyright © 2017 by Dennis Hunter

All rights reserved.

ISBN-10: 154685584X
ISBN-13: 978-1546855842

Image Usage
The crossed vajra or thunderbolt symbol, with triskelion in center, which appears on certain title pages, is licensed for use under the Creative Commons Attribution-Share Alike 4.0 International License. Artwork created by Madboy74. Cover image by Greg Rakozy.

Cover design by Dennis Hunter. Art direction and consulting by Juan-Carlos Castro.

Let me respectfully remind you:
Life and death are of supreme importance.
Time swiftly passes by and opportunity is lost.
Each of us should strive to awaken. Awaken!
Take heed! Do not squander your life.

— Traditional Zen chant

CONTENTS

	Acknowledgments	i
	Preface	1
	Stop Sleepwalking Through Your Life	10
	Introduction to the Four Reminders	19
I	**The First Reminder**:	31
	Appreciate your life. Do something meaningful with it.	
II	**The Second Reminder**:	53
	Life is short (and then you die). Don't waste time.	
III	**The Third Reminder**:	89
	You create your own reality. Make sure it's a good one.	
IV	**The Fourth Reminder**:	129
	Going in circles is pointless. Wake up!	
	Afterword	180
	Additional Resources	186

ACKNOWLEDGMENTS

I am profoundly grateful to my teachers Pema Chödrön and Dzogchen Ponlop for their guidance, inspiration, and instructions. Without their encouragement to deeply contemplate the Four Reminders and to write about them, this book would not exist.

The monastic community led by Pema Chödrön, where I lived as a Buddhist monk for two years, provided a cradled and supportive environment for writing and contemplation. One person in particular at the monastery, the monk Gelong Loden Nyima, has been a sounding board for ideas throughout the process of writing this book, and contributed some ideas of his own. I'm thankful to him for offering his wonderfully condensed impressions of the Four Reminders, including the phrase, "Going in circles is pointless." He kindly granted his permission to borrow that phrase when I was struggling to find a way to capture the elusive spirit of the Fourth Reminder in a pithy way.

This book has been over a decade in the making. Along the way I consulted and was inspired by a wide range of ancient and modern texts dealing with the Four Reminders. Dzogchen Ponlop's booklet *Turning Towards Liberation*, and his wise and mischievous teachings to me over the years, were the spark that started the fire. Patrul Rinpoche's *Words of My Perfect Teacher*, the Ninth Karmapa Wangchuk Dorje's *The Ocean of Definitive Meaning* (along with his liturgical texts), and Gampopa's *The Jewel Ornament of Liberation* all provided classical formulations and commentaries on the Four Reminders. Khandro Rinpoche's *This Precious Life*, Sakyong Mipham's *Turning the Mind into an Ally*, and Mingyur Rinpoche's *Turning Confusion into Clarity* offered more contemporary perspectives. I'm profoundly grateful to the unbroken lineage of Tibetan meditation masters who have been teaching and writing for a millennium about the Four Reminders. If this book contains any wisdom at all it is their wisdom, remixed to suit modern, Western minds. Any misunderstandings or mistakes are my own.

I'm grateful to the many friends and students who have patiently listened to me talking about this book for a decade, in workshops and in personal conversations, and for their insights and feedback on this deep and often sobering subject matter. I'm also profoundly thankful to the colleagues who read through the manuscript before publication and offered generous words of support, including Ethan Nichtern, Yogarupa Rod Stryker, Sensei Koshin Paley Ellison, and Kino MacGregor. (I've included their kind endorsements at the back of the book.)

And I'm thankful to my husband Adrian Molina, who illuminates my strengths when I feel weak, and calls out my nonsense when I need someone to call me out on it. Paradoxically, he encourages me to be my best self while discouraging me from taking myself too seriously – which, in a way, is what the Four Reminders are really about. Without his patient support and loving kindness, neither this book nor my previous book *You Are Buddha* would exist. For me, he is the Fifth Reminder.

PREFACE

Here are the facts:

- You are a spark of divine consciousness in human form. Your life is blessed, and full of purpose and potential.
- Your time is running out. You will die – and possibly sooner than you imagine. When death comes, everything you cling to and think of as important and meaningful will be stripped away.
- You are – and probably to a larger extent than you realize – the architect of your reality. Your actions, words and thoughts have consequences, shaping the lives and experiences of other people as well as your own. Everything you do matters.
- You have, within yourself, the will and the capacity to live a deeply meaningful, awakened life. But you won't find it in the familiar comforts of external things and experiences. Going in circles and chasing fulfillment on the outside is pointless. The fulfillment you seek can only come from within.

THE FOUR REMINDERS

Somewhere along the way, blinded by the whirlwind of daily life with its endless distractions and mirages, you have lost sight of these basic facts about yourself. The Four Reminders are a map to rediscovering these truths, an ancient guide to spiritual awakening that has been passed down in both oral and written form in the Tibetan Buddhist tradition for hundreds of years. Contemplating the Four Reminders is meant to help you remember these elemental truths and apply them to your own life. If you let them sink deep into your being, the Four Reminders will steer your life towards what is truly meaningful and carry you along the path to awakening. Think of the Four Reminders as jumper cables attached to a very ancient, very powerful battery, which will help you jump-start the engine of awakening in your own life.

If your life is already in perfect alignment with these four simple truths, then you probably don't need this book. You know how incredibly fortunate you are and take nothing for granted; you are using your life in the most effective and beneficial ways possible. Keenly aware of your own mortality, you know that the time and manner of your death are unpredictable and may come at any moment, so you don't waste time on trivial pursuits. Understanding that your actions, speech and thoughts shape your experience of the world and affect everyone else in your vicinity, you act and speak only in ways that will bring benefit and happiness and reduce suffering; therefore, your conscience is unblemished. And since you know for sure that no lasting or reliable security can be found in the glittering seductions of wealth, fame, power, possessions, relationships and other external things, you relate to these apparitions with equanimity and non-attachment. Instead of clinging and grasping at worldly comforts, you focus your energy on the treasure that lies within. You are living, day by day, ever more deeply as the expression and embodiment of the awakened wisdom and compassion that are the very core of your being, and you are bringing that wisdom and compassion to benefit a world that so desperately needs it.

If that describes you, then you may already be enlightened, or at least well on your way. You could stop here, if you like. This book is for the rest of us, who could use a little help pointing our lives in the general direction of awakening.

The Red Pill

Most of us spend our lives in a trance. We dream away our nights and sleepwalk through our days. We live ensnared in a vast web of distractions, obligations, and pinging devices that pull our attention constantly outward, all set against a backdrop of internal noise and mental chatter that we can never seem to quiet. Our minds and nervous systems are jammed with this noise and signal chaos, leaving us feeling confused and disconnected from ourselves. Once in a while, a pleasant or unpleasant shock startles us out of the trance, if only for a short time. We fall head over heels in love with someone, and life suddenly looks brilliant, sparkling, charged with positive energy that shakes us awake. "Wow!" we think, "I've never felt this alive before!"

Or the rug gets pulled out from under our feet in a less happy way: someone close to us dies, our marriage falls apart, or the doctor gives us a dreaded diagnosis, and life suddenly looks gloomy, menacing, charged with negative energy. Rattled by the turn of events, we pick ourselves up from the floor and look around, acutely aware of our own fragility as if learning about it for the first time. "Oh my God!" we say, "what am I doing with my life?" Forced to pause and take stock of all the shiny toys and peak experiences we've collected around us, we re-evaluate the sense of meaning we attributed to these things and find ourselves coming up short. Like the old Peggy Lee song, we ask: "Is that all there is?"

THE FOUR REMINDERS

We all ask ourselves Peggy Lee's question at one time or another. But for the most part, we don't dwell on it for very long, because we soon fall asleep again. It's easy to slip back into the comforting trance of distractions and illusions because it is so familiar and seductive, like a narcotic drug. We willingly lose ourselves again and again in the pursuit of ambition, material gain, validation, security, or mindless entertainment – and, in the process, we overlook the real treasure that already dwells inside our own hearts and minds.

The Four Reminders will appeal to you if – and only if – you are tired of being asleep; if you want to wake up and live a more meaningful life. These four simple contemplations are meant to dispel the illusions that drugged you into this lifelong trance in the first place. To use a modern medical analogy, imagine that your brain has receptors for ignorance and self-deception, but it also has receptors for wisdom. Like high-grade pharmaceuticals, the Four Reminders will begin to block your brain's receptors for ignorance and open its receptors for wisdom and clarity.

If you've seen the movie *The Matrix*, you may recall the scene in which Morpheus offers Neo the choice between a red pill or a blue pill. The Four Reminders are like the red pill, which awakened Neo to the harsh reality that lay hidden behind the dysfunctional but somehow comforting illusions of the Matrix. You *could* take the blue pill, put away this book, and go back to your comfortable fantasy life, asleep and cozy inside a vast, sinister machine of materialism, greed, and aggression that is sucking away your life energy to fuel what philosopher Rob Brezsny called "the sour, puckered mass hallucination that is mistakenly referred to as 'reality'." But if you have the courage to really seek out the truth, you will not take the blue pill; you will take the red pill and actually wake up.

It's your decision – no one is going to force either choice on you. But, like Neo, if you *do* choose the red pill, then you are granting your consent to have certain illusions taken away from you. You should be sure you are ready for that, and be committed to see the process through to completion.

In Tibetan Buddhism, the Four Reminders are also called the "Four Thoughts that Turn the Mind Towards the Dharma." *Dharma* is an ancient Sanskrit word with many meanings, but here it simply means "truth": the truth of how things actually are, as opposed to how they appear within the collective hallucination of so-called reality. Contemplating these four thoughts turns the mind towards the spiritual path that leads us out of confusion and into wisdom; out of lies and into truth; out of sleep and into waking up.

By definition, a reminder brings your attention back to something already known. These brief instructions are called "reminders" because they bring your mind back to four basic truths about your human existence that, deep down, you already know. Yet somehow you keep forgetting or denying them. Why? It's not as if the Four Reminders point to some great mystery, something esoteric and hidden. Quite the opposite, the truths they point to are rather simple and obvious. But we humans, in spite of our highly evolved intelligence (or maybe because of it), are very good at ignoring the obvious and forgetting simple truths.

Denial Is Not a River in Egypt
If you aren't convinced yet, consider this:

- Most of us are in denial about the preciousness of our human lives. We take life for granted and get lost in a maze of time-wasting distractions. We complain endlessly about what's wrong with our lives and pine for things we don't have. Never satisfied with what we have and where we are, we lean restlessly into the future, hoping for some magical resolution of our

problems in some fantastical moment that always seems to be just around the next corner. Sometimes, in extreme cases, this chronic sense of dissatisfaction even leads us down a path to self-destruction.
- Most of us are in denial about the reality of death, until death actually happens to us or to someone close to us. We go through life like we have all the time in the world, as if death were merely a theoretical possibility, something far in the future that we don't really need to think about right now. When death comes, which is often without warning and sooner than expected, we are taken by surprise and are full of regrets over all the things we have or have not done.
- Most of us are in denial about the effects of our actions. Clouded by self-centeredness and out of touch with our own moral compass, we prioritize our own comfort and happiness above that of others. We act in ways that are selfish, inconsiderate, or outright harmful. The consequences of our actions are carried outward, like a ripple effect, into the environment and into the future. By trying to ensure our own happiness, we ironically end up creating the causes for our own future suffering.
- Most of us are in denial about how much of our own suffering is actually self-created. We search misguidedly for meaning and security outside, in material things and in momentary experiences of pleasure that constantly slip through our fingers and leave us wanting more. We can spend our entire lives like this, going in pointless circles and chasing our own tails, until we collapse in despair or exhaustion.

Do you notice a pattern here? We are in *denial* of basic facts about our lives, and being in denial puts us at war with reality. The degree to which you conquer your own denial and make peace with reality is the degree to which you can wake up from the trance and become a happier,

INTRODUCTION

more effective human being. As long as you remain in denial, willfully ignorant of any aspect of reality, then you remain confused and asleep.

We create a lot of unnecessary suffering for ourselves this way. The Buddha taught that our suffering has a root cause, which is ignorance. Ignorance comes in two basic forms: *passive* and *active*. *Passive* ignorance is just not knowing about something, not being informed about it. This type of ignorance is simple to remedy through education and exposure to the facts. Once you know the facts, then you are no longer ignorant. But the second type of ignorance, *active* ignorance, is more pernicious and difficult to counteract.

Active ignorance comes into play when you slip into denial about something. You willfully turn a blind eye to it, forget about it, blot it out of awareness, and hide your head in the sand. In other words, you *ignore* it. Stuck in denial, you might be exposed to the truth again and again, but you won't hear it or let it sink in because you're determined not to. The truth could be right in front of your face, but you remain stuck in the fantasy world you've created for yourself.

This is why the Four Reminders are so helpful. It's not that you *don't already know* what they are telling you. If you scratch beneath the surface, you realize that you *do* know what they are telling you. In fact, what they are telling you is pretty obvious, once you look at it. It's just that, caught up in the trance as you are, *you would rather not think about these things*. That's called denial, the active form of ignorance.

The Four Reminders are not spiritual comfort food; there is nothing very comforting about them, just as there was nothing terribly comforting about the reality to which Neo awakened after taking the red pill. If you're looking for the next "Chicken Soup for the Soul," I regret to inform you that you have picked up the wrong book. Instead, you could think of the Four Reminders as four compassionate slaps in the face; four irritating pinpricks to goad you into being more alert; four glasses of cold water lovingly thrown in your face while you sleep, to startle you awake. They are designed to snap you out of the fog of delusions you've been living in, so that you can begin to relate to your life and your world with greater clarity and purpose. The aim of the Four Reminders is nothing less than to help you discover what it is that you are here on earth to do, and then to summon the courage and determination to begin doing exactly that.

In the Gnostic Gospel of Thomas, one of the earliest scriptures of Christianity, Jesus said, "Seek and do not stop seeking until you find. When you find, you will be disturbed. After being disturbed, you will be astonished, and will rule over the All."

I don't know about ruling over the All, but if you've picked up this book, you're already seeking. So now it's just a matter of not stopping. If you are ready to look within yourself and be a little bit disturbed, and then hopefully a little bit astonished, let's continue.

If that doesn't sound like something you're up for, then take the blue pill and go back to sleep. There are probably a dozen exciting, new "reality shows" on TV that you're missing at this very moment. Sweet dreams.

Think for Yourself

In a famous scripture, the Buddha said that we should not accept anything we are taught simply because it's passed down to us through tradition, or because it was written in a holy book, or because it was spoken by an esteemed person or spiritual teacher. Instead, we should deeply question and analyze what we hear, and explore it in our own experience. If, after sufficient testing, we find that it seems fundamentally true and leads to benefit and happiness, then we should accept it as truth and try to live in accordance with it. But if we find that it does not, then we should

INTRODUCTION

reject it and move on.

Please adopt the same approach to this book. Don't take anything written here at face value. Read it, absorb its message, reflect on it in your own time, and see if it stands up to the tests of reason and intuition. If something really doesn't make sense, then don't give it another thought. But if it strikes a chord in you and seems to express a meaningful truth, then take its message to heart and consider what living that truth might mean for you.

STOP SLEEPWALKING THROUGH YOUR LIFE

About 2,600 years ago, in the region of the world that we now call India, something so extraordinary happened that it altered the course of history and gave birth to one of the world's major religions, Buddhism.

For those in western countries, India has a reputation as an exotic and mystical place. It is, after all, the land that gave us men who play musical instruments to hypnotize cobras, and others who walk on hot coals and sleep on beds of nails. Even in today's India, it is not all that uncommon for people to give up everything and devote their entire lives to a spiritual quest – a land where, at this moment, some 13 million holy men called *saddhus* cover their naked or almost-naked bodies in ash and sit in meditation, sometimes for years on end, eating almost nothing, pushing the flesh and the mind to the limits of human endurance in a relentless quest for spiritual awakening.

And so it was nearly three thousand years ago, when our story takes place. Essentially what happened was this: a young prince from a well-placed, royal family, who had it all – youth, good looks, health, wealth, a beautiful wife, power, sex, romance, servants, and the promise of a future as king – *willingly* chose to give up his pampered life and set out as a beggar on a lonely and comfortless search for spiritual realization. Take a moment and let that sink in.

To put this in context, think of Hollywood's biggest blockbuster movie star (whoever that happens to be at the moment). Now try to imagine the uproar that would ensue if he suddenly abandoned his career, left his wife, gave away all his money, houses and possessions, shaved his head and put on tattered clothes, and left Hollywood behind to seek spiritual awakening alone in a cabin in the Alaskan wilderness. He did *whaaaat*? That would be the modern-day equivalent of what this young prince in India did.

Now, that was a strange and radical thing to do, but that alone wouldn't have altered world history. If that was all there was to this story, it wouldn't have changed anything except the young prince's life and the lives of his parents and his wife, all of whom were shocked and upset by his unthinkable decision to walk away from the luxurious, comfortable life he had shared with them in the palace.

But what happened next changed everything. After years of arduous, single-minded practice, the young man formerly known as a prince finally experienced the great spiritual awakening for which he had been searching: Enlightenment with a capital 'E.' It's said that he attained freedom from suffering by completely and permanently awakening from all delusions and misunderstandings about the nature of reality, seeing everything with total clarity.

He became known as the Buddha, which means the Awakened One, and after his awakening he started attracting students and followers and teaching about the spiritual path. Historians say that he taught for about 45 years, giving his students everything from the most practical, concrete instructions on how to live a moral life and how to meditate, to the highest philosophical views on the nature of mind and existence.

Among the very highest of these philosophical views was what he called "Buddha Nature." This teaching, which was the subject of my first book, *You Are Buddha*, says that awakened mind – brilliant and limitless and free – is actually your deepest nature. Like every other living creature, you already have it. You've never been without it; you could no more be without it than the sun could be without its light. Buddha Nature is not something you have to manufacture or create through spiritual practice, or be granted through the grace of some higher being. Your task on the spiritual path is to simply uncover this basic goodness, to reveal the radiant, awakened mind that is already there, waiting to be realized. Underneath all your confusion and neuroses, at your very core, Buddha – awakened mind and heart – is what you are.

Breaking Bad

This is a radically positive view of human nature, and if you are like most people, you may find it a bit hard to swallow. Why is that?

Well, to start with, it clashes with one of the core beliefs of the Abrahamic religions that saturate our society: the doctrine of Original Sin. That doctrine says that human nature is primordially corrupt, fallen from grace – you are *basically bad* rather than *basically good*. From the moment of birth, you are existentially and spiritually doomed, unless you seek out and receive the mercy of a deity who is regarded as being external to you. And this external deity is often depicted as petty, jealous, angry, capricious, punishing and vengeful. His mercy doesn't seem very forthcoming, unless you play your cards right and do everything by the rules. You must always walk on spiritual eggshells, fearful of being judged and condemned for making one false step.

This may not be everyone's experience of the Abrahamic religions, but speaking for myself, that's how it felt when I was indoctrinated, as a child, in the Southern Baptist church in Oklahoma.

If, like so many people, you are haunted by the doctrine of Original Sin, then the Buddha's notion of basic goodness may feel rather alien. Instead of feeling like you embody the dignity and wisdom and compassion of a Buddha, you often feel poverty-stricken, mired in low self-esteem, riddled with self-doubt, bogged down in depression, prone to panic attacks or fits of anger or self-pity, or mired in existential fears or neurotic worries about who you are and where you are going. Basic goodness is a nice-sounding theory – and you hope it's true – but frankly you're not sure if the theory holds water. Much of your everyday, lived experience seems to suggest otherwise.

Perhaps, when you hear about Buddha Nature or basic goodness, it clicks with something buried deep in your heart; you may feel some primal, intuitive inkling of its truth. But chances are, you identify much more readily and automatically with your neuroses and bad habits and confusion and discontentment – in short, with everything that is "wrong" with you and your life, and all the things that have ever gone wrong or could potentially go wrong. Basic goodness sounds appealing, in a warm and fuzzy way, but basic badness is much more familiar.

This *negativity bias* is deeply embedded in our society; it is part of our zeitgeist. Even though it is all around us, we are often blind to its effects – much like a fish is blind to the water in which it swims. From a neurobiological point of view, it is even encoded in our genes. We evolved to pay more attention to threats and problems than to opportunities and positive feelings, and for good reason. The members of the species who were alert to threats and attuned to their fears tended to survive and reproduce, while those who spaced out or moved too slowly were eaten by predators. Over time, the negativity bias became hardwired into our biology, a deeply ingrained pattern that's difficult to resist.

Stinking Thinking

The negativity bias has even seeped into modern psychology, clouding the way we study and think about the mind. In the last hundred years, Western psychology has produced libraries of books that focus on pathology and disease and insanity and neurosis and all that could possibly go wrong with the human mind. Psychology has also tried, in various, noble ways, to develop cures for the problems it diagnoses, and it has made remarkable progress in the treatment of mental disorders, particularly from a neurological perspective.

But, in those same hundred years, Western psychology has had precious little to say about what really constitutes a healthy, positive, fulfilled, and happy human mind. More recently, with the growth of 'positive psychology,' this has begun to change. Today researchers are working to define, quantify and increase human happiness. But in relative terms, there is a mountain of pathology and a molehill of positive psychology. Western psychology lags behind the Buddhist tradition in terms of articulating a vision of basic human goodness, which the Buddha taught nearly 2,600 years ago.

So the paradox we struggle with is that this radiant, awakened mind – which is said to be our most basic nature – doesn't feel natural to us. Although Buddha Nature may be there, somewhere within us, it remains hidden, encrusted beneath layer upon layer of confusion, misunderstanding, negative conditioning and sleep.

Sleep, in this case, does not mean a mind that is unconscious and blank. On the contrary, it refers to a mind that is overactive, neurotic, hallucinating, caught in a trance, completely distracted by its own internal chatter and external entertainments, lured outside of itself by shiny objects in its environment, and lost in schemes to manipulate and acquire those objects to make itself happy. Sound familiar?

When people begin to meditate, they are often shocked to discover how easily their minds get swept away in this trance of distractions. Sitting down with the intention to be still and quiet, they are suddenly confronted with the noise and restlessness in their own minds, as if encountering themselves for the first time. They glimpse what Buddhists call "monkey mind" – the untamed mind that jumps and screeches and refuses to be still. This experience can be so humbling and disorienting that people sometimes give up on meditation before they even have a chance to really get started.

The constant, channel-surfing blur of mental distraction and wildness is what keeps you out of touch with your basic goodness and out of sync with your own life, trapped in a confused state in which you misperceive reality. Acting out of that confused state, you try to secure happiness for yourself through various ill-conceived and misdirected efforts. You stumble through life trying to cobble together a security blanket of happiness from patches of material pleasure and comfort; but the blanket is always fraying at the edges, and the patches seem to disintegrate before your very eyes, even as you try desperately to fix them in place.

This is the real meaning of 'sleep.' The Tibetan teacher Chogyam Trungpa, who played a major role in bringing Tibetan Buddhism to the West, called this trance 'cocoon,' an image that suggests a habitual way of wrapping yourself up in your own snug security blanket of illusions. Living in your cocoon, you are totally caught up in the struggle of mundane existence, focused on yourself and what you think will make you happy. As if in a daze, you spin on your hamster wheel and imagine, mistakenly, that you're getting somewhere – unaware that there is a deeper dimension to life, something potentially more meaningful than material comforts and fleeting moments of pleasure.

THE FOUR REMINDERS

Asleep at the Wheel
Meanwhile, your life goes on without you, hurtling down the road like a vehicle in which you have fallen asleep at the wheel. You keep waking up, looking around with alarm at the scenery flashing by – *How did I get here? Where did the time go?* – and then falling back asleep. To each side, you see other people, also asleep at the steering wheels of their own lives. To your left, someone veers off the road, crashes, and dies in a fireball without ever waking up. To your right, someone else quietly runs out of fuel and putters to a stop; quickly left behind, they are soon forgotten in the forward rush of life. And there are others, still, who zoom past you on the road, people who appear to know where they are going and what they are doing. Maybe they do. Maybe they don't.

If you are like most people, you have been asleep at the wheel of your life for as long as you can remember. Perhaps you can recall a few bright moments, especially when you were young, of being awake at the wheel, and looking around with astonishment – but back then you weren't fully in control. Your little toy car was still attached by tow-ropes to your parents' larger vehicles, and they made your driving decisions for you. As you grew up, you bucked and struggled against your tow-ropes, and you swore that when you were finally old enough to drive your own car, you would make better driving decisions than your parents had made.

Stopping the Freight Train
Coming out of a long and habitual sleep is not necessarily pleasant or easy. It is irritating and humbling and scary to wake up at the wheel of your life and realize that you are hurtling forward in time with only a vague, intermittent, and dream-like idea of who you are and where you are going. To wake up from that sleep, you have to be willing to face some unpleasant facts: in the process, "you will be

disturbed," as Jesus said in the Gnostic Gospels. It's a lot less disturbing to just stay asleep. Sleep – the all-consuming blur of life's distractions and illusions – is a familiar pattern. There is a certain comfort in the familiar, dysfunctional though it may be. It is a lifelong habit with a lot of energy and momentum behind it, and that momentum is not easy to break.

Imagine a very long freight train with many cars stretching into the horizon. Each of those cars represents one whole year of your life. Breaking the momentum of such a long train and bringing it to a stop requires a tremendous amount of applied energy or friction. With a freight train's huge mass and momentum, you don't just suddenly bring it to a stop like you do with an automobile or a bicycle. You plan ahead and start applying the brakes early, a mile or two ahead of where you want to actually stop.

You apply the brakes by working with your mind and chipping away, bit by bit, at the momentum of your own confusion. Eventually, you will be able to stop the train and turn your mind completely back in the direction from which you came – towards the primordial wisdom of awakened mind that is, according to the Buddha, the heart of all beings and the origin of all things.

The Four Reminders help you begin to put the brakes on your confusion and turn your mind back towards the source of your being, the truth of your inherent awakened potential. When manifesting that awakened potential becomes the number-one priority in your life, then the Four Reminders will have served their purpose, which is to turn your mind away from sleep and towards awakening; away from attachment to mundane comforts and trivial pursuits and towards a life of meaning; away from self-deception and towards truth.

On the spiritual path, as in life, the results you get depend on your intentions and aspirations, and the effort you apply towards realizing them. With a clear and strong

THE FOUR REMINDERS

intention to wake up and to be of service in the world by helping others wake up, then even mundane activities like sweeping the floor or cleaning toilets can be a path to awakening. But with the wrong motivation, with a mind bogged down in ignorance and materialism and stuck in habitual patterns, then even the loftiest, most advanced spiritual practices are, to quote a not-so-delicate line from the esteemed 18th-century Tibetan yogi Patrul Rinpoche, "good-for-nothing goat shit."[1]

---

[1] From Patrul Rinpoche's verses on meditation and the spiritual path, *Advice from Me to Myself*.

INTRODUCTION TO
THE FOUR REMINDERS

1

Appreciate your life.
Do something meaningful with it.

2

Life is short (and then you die).
Don't waste time.

3

You create your own reality.
Make sure it's a good one.

4

Going in circles is pointless.
Wake up!

THE FOUR REMINDERS

**The First Reminder:
Appreciate your life.
Do something meaningful with it.**

If you are like most people, you live in a habitual poverty mentality – feeling like *things just aren't good enough*. You so often take your life and your positive circumstances for granted, failing to appreciate how fortunate you are. You also have a deeply ingrained habit of dwelling on the negative: what you lack and what isn't right about your circumstances.

But the First Reminder doesn't ask you to just put on a smile and be happy, in a Pollyanna sort of way; it challenges you to recognize how fortunate you actually are, and what a miraculous opportunity you have *right now*. When you dwell habitually on the negative, or waste your life pursuing goals that are less than meaningful, you don't take full advantage of the precious opportunity you have *here and now* to wake up from the trance.

**The Second Reminder:
Life is short (and then you die).
Don't waste time.**

You assume that there's no big urgency about this business of waking up. You always think you have lots of time left, until suddenly you don't. Through contemplating the Second Reminder, let the truth of death and impermanence sink into your bones in order to shake you out of your complacency and remind you of the reality that your life (even under the best of circumstances) is very short.

Death is unpredictable and may come without warning at any time. Developing a keen awareness of the impermanence of everything – and especially your own mortality – spurs you to live with urgency and a heightened sense of purpose.

The Third Reminder:
You create your own reality.
Make sure it's a good one.

You are born, and you live and die, in a vast web of cause and effect, or "karma." Everything you think, say and do ripples outward and has consequences. Everything you do either brings more peace and clarity into the world and helps you wake up from the trance; or it brings more suffering and disappointment into the world and keeps you sleepwalking through life, always stumbling over the consequences of your actions.

Like a magician, everything you do conjures a result in your life, even if you don't necessarily see the result at the time you commit the action. Karma isn't always a bitch – but it certainly can be, if you aren't mindful. You should pay attention to the seeds you sow in every moment – because you will eventually, inevitably, reap what you sow.

The Fourth Reminder:
Going in circles is pointless.
Wake up!

The external pleasures and comforts of this world are fleeting and illusory, like a mirage. And yet you behave as if you truly believe that lasting, reliable happiness and security can be found in such things. You look for meaning by grasping tightly at material objects, experiences and relationships, and in doing so, you only cause yourself further suffering, amplifying your feelings of insecurity and loss. Ancient Tibetan texts describe this behavior as "licking honey from a razor blade."

You cause yourself so much unnecessary suffering through your attachment to such things. Ask yourself this: if you were on your deathbed at this very moment, would you feel content that you had spent your life as meaningfully as you could – or would you feel regret, having wasted too much time on the hamster wheel of career and ambition, pursuing material objects and experiences that, in the end, only left you feeling empty and hollow? Seen in the light of what's really meaningful, what are your priorities?

Four Essential Points

Over the centuries, these four essential points have been expressed in various forms by many legendary Tibetan yogis and teachers. One of the earliest written versions of the Four Reminders appeared in verse form in the 16th century, as part of a liturgical text written by His Holiness the 9th Karmapa, Wangchuk Dorje. Other ritual texts articulating the Four Reminders were penned by Tibetan meditation masters like Jigme Lingpa, Jamgön Kongtrül, and His Holiness Dilgo Khyentse Rinpoche. Regardless of how they are phrased, the core ideas expressed in the Four Reminders appear throughout the canon of scriptures attributed to the Buddha, and always boil down to these four points: appreciating the preciousness of human life, remembering the reality of impermanence and death, understanding the inescapable law of karma, and acting on the urgency of breaking free from the habitual causes of suffering and turning towards freedom and peace.

The phrasing of the Four Reminders here, in this book, is my own – with the exception of the Fourth Reminder, captured in a pith phrase as "Going in circles is pointless" by my friend, the Shambhala Buddhist monk Loden Nyima. Rather than quoting the Four Reminders from an ancient liturgical text, I felt it was important with this book to put these four essential points into fresh, uncomplicated English, and to explain their meaning in a way that will hopefully resonate with you and make sense to you regardless of whether or not you have any previous study of Tibetan Buddhism.

INTRODUCTION TO THE FOUR REMINDERS

This particular approach to explaining the Four Reminders – in simple, everyday terms – was inspired by what Albert Einstein once said: "You don't really understand something unless you can explain it to your grandmother."

There have been other published books and articles about the Four Reminders, including some by great teachers whom I deeply admire and respect. But if you were to put one of those traditional texts in front of your grandmother, she would have a hard time understanding it and relating to the subject, simply because of the way those books tend to rely on the reader's familiarity and comfort level with Tibetan Buddhist religion and philosophy.

The Buddha's essential wisdom that was distilled, centuries ago, into the Four Reminders remains as relevant to our lives today as it ever was. But over time, that wisdom has been veiled within many layers of Tibetan cultural tradition, religious practices, and a thicket of hand-me-down explanatory metaphors that have been repeated across the centuries. These metaphors, no doubt, made perfect sense when they were first written, in the light of lamps burning yak butter, by monks living in the feudalistic, agrarian society of old Tibet. But what made perfect sense in feudal Tibet in the 16th century doesn't always make perfect sense in the 21st-century, in a completely different cultural context.

Although there is nothing particularly esoteric about the Four Reminders, the traditional texts in which the Four Reminders appeared were indeed esoteric, and intended for a rather restricted audience of highly committed students. These texts often formed the liturgies for what is called *ngöndro*, which means "the preliminaries." *Ngöndro* refers to a range of practices that are performed by students during the preliminary stages of initiation into the Tantric Buddhist path. In classical *ngöndro*, students might be required to perform 100,000 physical prostrations, repeat a complex mantra in Sanskrit 100,000 times while

THE FOUR REMINDERS

holding an elaborate visualization in the mind, perform 100,000 ceremonial offerings, and complete 100,000 repetitions of a devotional prayer. Depending on a student's level of enthusiasm and the amount of time they are able to commit to it, *ngöndro* may take months or years to complete.

Obviously, such elaborate ceremonial and religious practices are not everyone's cup of tea. For those who are interested in studying the Four Reminders in the traditional context of *ngöndro*, there are other books written by qualified Tantric masters and lineage holders of Tibetan Buddhism. (Refer to the Acknowledgments section of this book for some suggestions.)

This book takes a somewhat different approach, which is to peel away the layers of cultural baggage and religious dogma that have accumulated around the Four Reminders over the centuries, and to illuminate their wisdom in a fresh, contemporary light. My hope here is to make the Four Reminders accessible to everyone – especially to those who have not deeply studied Buddhist philosophy, and who may have no interest in religious practices like *ngöndro*. I've tried to explain the Four Reminders, in other words, in a way that Einstein's proverbial grandmother – or yours – would understand and find useful.

If devoted Tantric students who are engaged in *ngöndro* also find this book useful, then that's a happy bonus. But it was not written with those students in mind, and it does not explain the Four Reminders in the context of such religious practices.

This book was written with *you* in mind, and it positions the Four Reminders in the context of nothing more religious than your life. By which I mean, your actual, daily, nitty-gritty life: your body, your thoughts and emotions, your work and career, your relationships, your family, your possessions. And by which I also mean, your "Life" in a more existential sense: your birth, your living, your death, and what it all means in the larger scheme of things.

After all, the purpose of the Four Reminders is to transform the way you see and relate to your life, and to re-orient your mind in the direction of awakening and living the most meaningful life you possibly can – a life on which you can look back, at the moment of death, and feel no pangs of regret. That sort of transformation doesn't come from rituals or ceremonies; it comes from looking deeply into your own experience and facing up to certain basic truths you've been trying to avoid for most of your life. And then asking yourself, once you've got hold of the truth, "Okay, now what?"

How to Work with This Book

The knowledge you can get merely from books is hollow compared to the knowledge that comes from your own informed, personal contemplation and experience. Books can give you lots of well-thought-out, nicely articulated ideas and theories about truth. But ideas and theories – if they are not used to get at the actual *experience* of truth – can actually become just another part of the trance, another part of what keeps you asleep. When circumstances come along that challenge you – when life throws you one of those upsetting curveballs – intellectual theories and ideas blow away like dust, and you learn with dismay how unreliable they are.

But when you discover through deepening contemplation how a timeless spiritual truth applies in your own experience – when you feel the "click" of intuitive insight as something deep within you responds in the affirmative, and when that truth begins to guide your life and your decisions – then that is the birth of genuine wisdom. Through that process, you start to develop a more reliable kind of understanding that will not blow away with a sudden change in circumstance.

You could skim through this book like a thousand

others, and you might find its message inspirational – but it probably wouldn't sink in very deeply. The way to work most effectively with the Four Reminders – the way to ignite the process of awakening – is to actually contemplate them. This means first hearing what the Four Reminders are saying, and then sitting with it and reflecting on how it resonates – or not – with your own experience. Does it seem true? If it seems true, does the truth disturb you in some way, and if so, what is behind that feeling of disturbance? How does the truth apply to your life, practically speaking, at the nitty-gritty, kitchen-sink level? Are you living in a way that reflects your understanding of the truth, or in a way that contradicts it?

In Tibetan, one of the words for meditation is *gom*, which means "familiarization" or "getting used to" something. Part of the effect of contemplation is simply familiarizing yourself with the truth and getting used to it, after a long time spent looking away from it. It's as if you've been living alone in the forest, for years, with no mirror to see yourself. The process of contemplation is like slowly re-discovering your own face in the mirror. Your face was always there, but you forgot what it looked like; you were not familiar with it.

Following each section of the book, there are suggested contemplations to help you explore and unpack the meaning of each of the Four Reminders in your own experience. Spend some time sitting with these contemplations. Don't rush through them. They are your opportunity to allow your own inherent wisdom, which has fallen asleep, to re-awaken.

For additional suggestions on working with the Four Reminders in contemplation and daily life, refer to the book's accompanying Study and Discussion Guide, which you can download for free at:

www.TheFourReminders.com

INTRODUCTION TO THE FOUR REMINDERS

How I Came to Write This Book

The Four Reminders have been in my life since 2002, when I began to study meditation and philosophy at a Shambhala Buddhist meditation center in New York City. A couple of years later, I became a student of the Tibetan teacher Dzogchen Ponlop, and one of the first instructions he gave me as his student was to thoroughly contemplate the Four Reminders.

What Dzogchen Ponlop asked me to do, specifically, was to spend eight weeks contemplating the Four Reminders as part of my daily meditation practice – two weeks on each reminder. At the end of each two-week segment, I was to write a short essay summarizing my personal viewpoint and insights into that particular reminder. I discovered that the simple act of writing down my insights, as if I had to explain the Four Reminders to someone else – to my grandmother, for example! – took my practice to a different place.

It wouldn't suffice to simply parrot what I had read in a book, or to repeat what I had heard my teacher say, or to rely on old explanatory metaphors handed down through the centuries. What I was challenged to do, instead, was to look within and discover my own understanding of the Four Reminders: to see how they applied to my lived experience, and to explain their meaning in my own words. The short essays I sent to my teacher in response to that assignment became the seeds that – after several more years of nurturing and contemplation – would eventually grow into this book.

In 2009 I felt a radical calling to deepen my spiritual search. I quit my job, sold or gave away most of my belongings, and went to live for two years as a Buddhist monk at a remote monastery in the rugged wilds of Cape Breton, Nova Scotia. There, under the guidance of another of my teachers, Pema Chödrön, and swaddled in saffron robes to ward off the brutal Canadian winters, I practiced various forms of meditation for several hours per day (including the esoteric practices of *ngöndro*, in which one begins each session by contemplating the Four Reminders).

And I wrote. I would often wake at 4:00am in order to get in an hour or two of writing before I was required to be in the meditation hall along with the other monks and nuns for morning chants. I wrote much of the material in this book while living at the monastery. I revisited the short essays I had written on the Four Reminders several years earlier, and rewrote them, and rewrote them again, and expanded upon them until they began to resemble the basic shape of this book. But it would still be several more years before the book would change again, taking its current form.

My time in the monastery was a blessing for me – especially the time spent in the presence of my teacher, Pema Chödrön – but it was not to last forever. I had come to the monastery without a plan, open to the possibility of remaining there permanently if I felt called to follow the life path of a Buddhist monk. But after two years of life in an isolated religious institution, I felt a calling to return to 'civilian' life in the outside world.

I moved back to New York City, and very quickly the manuscript about the Four Reminders went on the back burner. It remained there for the next few years, while I found my bearings and re-adjusted to life outside the monastery. Ironically, during this time, I could see myself getting a little too caught up in some of the 'worldly' things – jobs, relationships, entertainment, and so on – that the Fourth Reminder warns about. But at the same time, after having been cloistered away in the monastery for two years, I also welcomed the opportunity to be back among the familiar comforts and pitfalls of 'worldly' life.

When I finally did return to the manuscript of this book, I was not happy with it at all. My time away from it, and the life experiences that shaped my perspective in the meantime, had totally changed my point of view about

INTRODUCTION TO THE FOUR REMINDERS

how the Four Reminders should be presented. Essentially, what I had written up to that point was still a rather traditional take on the Four Reminders, with lots of quotes and references to classical Tibetan Buddhist liturgies and commentaries. But what I really wanted to do was to make these wisdom teachings fresh and contemporary and accessible to anyone, regardless of whether or not they had any previous study of Tibetan Buddhism or any interest in things like *ngöndro*.

And so I began to rewrite the book once again. I dramatically altered its approach and tone, stripping away layer after layer of religious jargon and unnecessary references to traditional texts and explanations. I kept returning to Einstein's provocation: putting myself in my grandmother's shoes, I tried to imagine if what I had written about the Four Reminders would make sense to her. If it seemed like it wouldn't, then I still needed to contemplate it more deeply and find another way of expressing it.

To articulate the wisdom of the Four Reminders in a way that's widely relevant to people's needs today, I had to stop relying so much on tradition and finally do what Dzogchen Ponlop had asked me to do all those years ago: look inside, search for the essence of the Four Reminders in my own understanding, and articulate that understanding in my own words. This book is the result of that effort.

May it serve as the spark that ignites your own fire of awakening (or as the red pill, if you prefer to stick with metaphors from *The Matrix*).

THE FIRST REMINDER

**APPRECIATE YOUR LIFE.
DO SOMETHING
MEANINGFUL WITH IT.**

APPRECIATE YOUR LIFE

Let's begin with a thought experiment. If you're reading or listening to this book, chances are pretty good that you're a human being – after all, dogs and horses and fish don't read books. You've been a human for as long as you can remember, so it might be difficult at this point for you to really imagine being anything else. But take a moment now and try to imagine it. What if you had actually been born into this world as a cat or a dog or a horse or a fish, instead of a human? Or, to think a little further outside the box, imagine you were born as some hideous creature with tentacles and horns and 33 eyes, living alone in a cave on a scorched and dusty planet orbiting another star in another galaxy, so far away that we humans with our feeble telescopes could not possibly know of its existence.

If, instead of being yourself as you are now, you were born as any of these other creatures, things would be very different for you. You might be lucky enough to have a normal lifespan, assuming you could find enough to eat and drink, and you didn't get eaten by another creature. If you were extremely lucky, you might even manage to reproduce, assuming you could find a mate. But beyond meeting these primal needs for survival – eating, sleeping, excreting and reproducing – what else would your life be about? Aside from licking your fur to clean yourself, what sort of opportunities do you imagine you would have for personal development and spiritual growth?

We humans may be the most gifted creatures on the planet, in terms of our intellectual capacities and evolutionary potential. Yet we often fail to appreciate our great potential and don't make good use of it. Forgetting how gifted we are, we spend much of our time complaining about all the large and small ways that life and other people disappoint us.

Of course you have your problems, your particular reasons for experiencing pain and suffering. You never get everything you want in life; and you have to put up, at times, with things or situations that you don't want and can't seem to get rid of. But in terms of having the circumstances you need for waking up from the trance – for putting the brakes on confusion and turning the freight train of the mind back towards its source – this human life you are living right now really couldn't get much better.

The Miracle of a Human Life

To start with, think about your body for a moment. Maybe it gives you problems or pains, or it has fallen ill; or maybe you're getting older, your blood pressure is high, or your joints ache. Maybe your body – which used to seem so dependable – just doesn't work as well as it used to. Or maybe you just don't like the way it looks: it's too fat or too skinny, too wrinkled, too tall or too short, too light or too dark. If you're like most people, you're probably not satisfied with your body as it is. It could always be *better*.

But consider how amazing, how unlikely, how fortunate it is to exist in the body you inhabit right now. An unbroken chain of miraculous circumstances stretching back millions of years – billions of years, in fact, to the explosions of stars and the formation of the world in which you live – has brought you into existence in this body, and each moment you are alive is a continual unfolding of those miracles. And yet how often do you stop to appreciate the marvel of your human body and all the things it makes possible for you?

Inside your chest is a heart that continually contracts and expands in order to pump blood through every cubic inch of your body. It has been doing this since long before you were actually born, and it will continue doing so until the day you die. Your heart beats non-stop, whether or not you ever think about it, approximately 50 million times per year. You also have lungs that breathe for you, effortlessly – on average, 15 times per minute, 900 times per hour, 21,000 times per day. You don't have to think about it or consciously control your breathing – although, curiously enough, you *can* if you want to.

You have 45 miles of nerve fibers running throughout your body, transmitting electrochemical signals from your scalp to the soles of your feet, to help you sense and interact with your world and all the beings and objects in it, to move about, to experience sensations and perceptions. You probably have eyes and ears and hands that work fairly well. You can do something like holding a book in your hands, a deceptively simple action that is the apex of millions of years of primate evolution.

But that's not all. Any monkey could hold a book. Unlike the monkey, you can also *read* it. That is a skill, and a gift, shared by no other species on earth. When you were a child, many adults worked hard on your behalf to transmit that evolutionary knowledge to you. In fact, millions of people have labored for thousands of years to develop and transmit this knowledge and ability from generation to generation so that you could be reading or listening to this book right now.

Because you were given this gift, your mind can recognize and interpret sounds and coded symbols of language with astonishing ease, and communicate with other minds using the same codes. Your mind is also capable of absorbing and processing complex ideas and thinking in abstract ways.

And, not least of all, your mind is endowed with the extraordinary gift of self-awareness: not only can you *know* things, but you can also *know that you know things*. You can *observe* what is happening in your own mind, as it's happening, which is what makes meditation possible.

You can think, and feel, and communicate. You can fall in love. You can learn algebra, or write poetry. You can make guacamole. You can sing and dance. You can evaluate complex situations and make rational decisions. Beyond those things, you are also blessed with an incredible, intuitive knowledge of your innate potential and a bold aspiration to follow the path of awakening. That aspiration is what led you to pick up this book in the first place. Contemplate the power of the magnanimous blessings that have been bestowed upon you, and make a solemn vow to yourself that you will never again wallow in the mud of doubt and self-pity.

You don't even have to imagine yourself as a cat or a dog or a horse or a fish or an alien on another planet. To understand how blessed you are, think of how many other humans on this small and increasingly distressed planet never enjoy the opportunities that you do. So many people in the world are starving and struggling just to survive from day to day. So many people spend their whole lives in places perpetually torn apart by warfare and violence, living always in fear – or fleeing across borders, living as refugees, running in terror towards any unfamiliar place that might offer them safety and survival. In terms of outer, material circumstances, the simple truth is that many people in the world don't feel nearly as safe and secure and comfortable as you do. They certainly don't have the luxury of indulging in books about personal growth or spiritual awakening. They are too busy trying to keep themselves and their loved ones out of harm's way. If you've never had to worry about such things, you are among the lucky few.

Many people in our society live in privileged bubbles of material comfort, without ever realizing it. Surrounded by beauty, fame, money, mansions, cars, and all the badges of status and achievement, hypnotized by shiny objects and lulled into the trance of pleasure, they have no inclination to look beneath the surface or to seek meaning in their human experience. It never occurs to them that there could be a deeper dimension to life.

You probably spend a lot of time complaining about your circumstances and pining for things you think would make your life better. But take a step back and look at all the other ways the chips could have fallen. Consider how fortunate you are to have precisely the life that you are living right now, and no other. It's not about how comfortable or secure you are in your outer circumstances, but how blessed you are with the conditions that are conducive to spiritual practice and awakening.

These miraculous gifts are some of the qualities that make it possible for you to wake yourself up from the trance and to ask Peggy Lee's nagging, eternal question: "Is that all there is?"

This is what the First Reminder means by appreciating your human life. In the larger scheme of things, such a blessed and fortunate life is incredibly rare. If you fail to see this, it's only because you don't usually look at your life from the larger scheme of things. You tend to focus myopically on what is right in front of your nose, thinking about what's wrong with you or with the people around you or with your circumstances, and scheming about ways to improve things. Lost in your schemes, you miss the big picture: the beauty and preciousness of your very own human existence, available here and now, for a limited time only.

When you take the preciousness of your human life for granted, you squander its value and fail to make the best use of it. And before you know it, as the Second Reminder will show, it will all be gone.

The Truth of Suffering

In the very first teaching he gave after awakening, the Buddha explained that life is riddled with suffering. The ancient Pali word he used for this, *dukkha*, is thought to refer to the way a potter's wheel screeches and wobbles when it's off-balance, or the way a wagon lurches and wobbles uncomfortably when one of its wheels is out of alignment.

The Buddha described *dukkha* in several ways. One of these is what he called *all-pervasive suffering*: a kind of gnawing undercurrent of psychological suffering that seems to haunt us everywhere we turn in life. We might experience this suffering in various ways: as fear, self-doubt, or restless dissatisfaction. Often, our experience of all-pervasive suffering leads us into patterns of self-criticism and criticism of others.

Even when our life situation is fundamentally good – almost perfect, in fact – we tend to dwell obsessively upon what we lack, and the ways in which we perceive ourselves or others to be deficient. The Buddhist teacher Tara Brach calls this habitual pattern "the trance of unworthiness." This trance is such a deep part of our conditioning that we rarely see it for the toxic cloud it actually is. We go about our lives as if this were normal, breathing in its dark fumes and exhaling them into our relationships and our world.

As mentioned earlier, Original Sin – the idea that something is wrong with us at the core, that we are primordially corrupt – leads us into a compulsive search for salvation from outside. We are forever trying to figure out what we could do or become or acquire in order to make ourselves worthy of redemption.

The Buddha taught a radically different idea. The fundamental nature of all beings, he said, is not corrupt,

THE FOUR REMINDERS

but basically good, primordially pure. Every person has the potential (given the proper guidance and conditions) to awaken to this true nature through the innate power of his or her own awareness. Life is fundamentally worth living, not for our hopes for the future, but for this very moment right now: what we already are and what we already have.

The path of awakening is not about fixing ourselves or manipulating our circumstances. It's about letting go of that compulsion, relaxing into our basic nature – coming back home to the goodness, the sanity, and the wholeness that are our true nature. In the yogic tradition this is called *santosha*: resting in a state of contentment, freed from the bondage of always seeking fulfillment and meaning on the outside.

If you are habitually caught up in self-criticism, doubt and discontent, it might be difficult for you to believe that your basic nature is fundamentally good, sane, and whole. It's hard for you to relax with yourself as you are and to be content in the present moment, because you are conditioned to fixate on *what could be* or *what should be* rather than *what is*. Your aversion to the present moment makes you speedy and impatient, obsessed with the future, restless and eager to be somewhere other than where you are, doing something other than what you are doing right now. This is an aspect of the all-pervasive suffering described by the Buddha.

I recall discovering this for myself, in a rather vivid way, when I first embarked upon my path of meditation many years ago. I enrolled in a series of intensive weekend meditation workshops that required long, grueling hours of sitting meditation, interspersed with short periods of walking meditation to stretch the legs. I spent the majority of those days trying unsuccessfully to keep my attention on the breath and feeling like a big failure at meditation.

After a few days of this self-torture, I had a sudden moment of clarity that almost made me burst out laughing. I realized that when I was sitting, I couldn't wait to stand up and walk again. And when I was walking, I couldn't wait to sit down again. I saw my own mind's habit of always leaning into the next moment, the next moment, and the next moment.

"How absurd!" I thought. "How can I be present with what's happening in this moment if I'm constantly waiting for the next moment, and imagining that it will be better than this one?"

If you let patterns of restlessness, discontent and self-criticism control your mind, they become a veil that prevents you from appreciating the precious opportunity you have for awakening in this life. Giving in to these ancient patterns and indulging them not only frustrates your emotional well-being but also stifles your spiritual growth.

But here's the good news: you can break the habit. Negative cycles of thought and emotion have no inherent solidity, no reality apart from what you give to them. Because you believe so much in your thoughts, they have power over you. You are the one who keeps the patterns spinning – and you also have the ability to stop doing that, at any moment you choose. You always have a choice between the red pill and the blue pill. You can always unplug from the Matrix and wake up from the trance.

THE GOLDILOCKS ZONE

In a classic children's fable, an adorable, pint-sized home invader named Goldilocks chances upon a house in the woods that's inhabited by a family of three bears. The bears are away from the house at the moment, so Goldilocks decides to sit down at their dining table and sample the porridge in their bowls. The first bowl of porridge is too hot; the second bowl is too cold; but the third bowl is just right, so she eats it all. She becomes sleepy after eating, so she decides to try out their beds. The first bed is too hard; the second bed is too soft; but the third bed feels just right, so Goldilocks lies down in it and takes a nap.

We are all a bit like Goldilocks. We have situations and experiences in life that are too hard, too hot, too difficult, too riddled with suffering. And we have other situations and experiences that are too soft, too cool, too easy, lulling us into a false sense of comfort or complacency. The ideal situation for us is somewhere in the middle – not too hot or too cold, not too hard or too soft.

In Tibetan Buddhist temples and books, you can see painted illustrations of what is called the Wheel of Life, depicting the Six Realms of Existence. From one point of view these six realms are regarded as actual places or dimensions inhabited by real beings. We can see two of these, the human and animal realms, with our eyes, but the other four realms are ethereal and invisible. But from another point of view all of the six realms simply describe six states of mind through which we constantly cycle. Sometimes we get stuck in one realm or another because our psychological state becomes fixed in that particular way of seeing the world.

In traditional depictions of the six realms of existence, our human realm is sort of like the Goldilocks zone – the realm that's "just right." Being human brings the right balance of opportunity and challenge, of pleasure and pain, because the human realm lies right in the middle of the spectrum of possibilities. At the lowest end of the spectrum are hell realms, which are like nightmares full of suffering and fear; at the highest end of the spectrum are god realms, which are like sweet dreams full of pleasure and bliss. If you have to be born somewhere, Tibetan Buddhists say, the best realm to be born into is the human realm, because it's here – where we are right now – that the balance of elements is "just right" for awakening from the trance.

The six realms – gods, jealous gods, humans, animals, hungry ghosts, and hell beings – paint a vivid picture of a spectrum of possible experiences, from the most torturous moments of suffering to the most exalted feelings of bliss. We will look at these realms again in the chapter on the Fourth Reminder, but here is a brief overview.

Hell Realms
In the hell realms, the intensity of suffering is so great that there's no time to think about anything else. The beings who are trapped there suffer seemingly endless physical and psychological torment. Subject to constant violence, pain, and terror, they are consumed by their own suffering.

Their only thought is the wish to escape it. This is actually how many people in our world today are forced to live.

Untold millions of human beings live in places of perpetual war and violence; others are held in captivity and exploited through human trafficking and forced prostitution. Perhaps you have never paused to consider it, but take a moment to appreciate how fortunate you are if you were born free from such overwhelming situations of extreme suffering.

Hungry Ghosts

The beings called 'hungry ghosts' are said to suffer constantly from extreme hunger and thirst, but they are cursed with bodies that make it impossible for them to take in the nourishment they yearn for. As in the Greek myth of Tantalus, they are tormented by seeing the objects of their hunger and thirst but never being able to enjoy them.

Most of us have experienced this state of mind in one form or another: the pain of unrequited love, which can never be satisfied, or the pain of addiction, which leads us in circles of suffering from which it becomes difficult to escape. Like hell-beings, hungry ghosts aren't free to pursue the path of awakening, because all their time is spent yearning for things they cannot have, and agonizing over the fact that they cannot get enough of them.

Animals

The animal realm is closer to the human realm, but Tibetan Buddhists still consider it an unfavorable place to be born. Animals can make wonderful, loving companions, and exhibit admirable qualities such as loyalty and compassion and playfulness. They also have certain kinds of intelligence and physical senses that may be sharper and more perceptive than our own.

But in terms of self-actualization and being able to truly wake up from the trance, an animal's options are pretty limited. The life of most animals is focused on day-to-day survival: eating and not being eaten, and hopefully reproducing if the opportunity presents itself. They cannot comprehend or communicate abstract ideas. Animals don't generally look for the meaning in things, and they cannot ask Peggy Lee's question, "Is that all there is?" (unless it's wondering whether all the food is gone).

Gods and Demi-Gods

In the celestial god realms, Tibetan Buddhists say, life is a bowl of cherries. Everyone has long, luxurious and comfortable lives, and everything they could possibly desire is available to them in abundance, as soon as they think about it. But because everything is so comfortable and perfect, the gods are lulled into a false sense of security. It's like a dream you wouldn't want to wake up from because the dream is so pleasant.

But a pleasant dream is no more real than an unpleasant one. None of the six realms are permanent, and the day inevitably comes when the good karma that landed beings in the god realm runs out. At that point, there is nowhere for them to go but down, towards a rude awakening in one of the lower realms. And so the 'wheel of life' keeps turning.

Of course this happens all the time, right here in our human realm. Our 'gods' are the celebrities whom we put on pedestals and worship; they are rich and famous and beautiful and popular. But we love to see them fall from their heavenly perches, a fact you can verify with a glance at the lurid headlines and photos on the covers of tabloid magazines in the supermarket. "MOVIE STAR IN CRISIS, GAINS 50 POUNDS!" reads one headline, beneath an unflattering photo of the star in question. "POP STAR'S MARRIAGE RUINED AS HUSBAND

CHEATS WITH OTHER POP STAR!" reads another.

Just below the god realm in classical Buddhist iconography is the realm of the demi-gods. The beings here are also called "jealous gods," because they look up at the god realm above them and feel pangs of jealousy. The gods seem to have better, easier lives than they do, with more pleasure and comfort and security. The jealous gods feel envious of this, and they constantly pick fights and wage war on the gods in order to try to get what they have. Sound familiar?

The Joy and Terror of Being Human

Tibetan Buddhists say that we are extremely fortunate to be where we are, in the Goldilocks zone of the human realm. We are not burdened by the all-consuming anguish experienced by hell-beings or hungry ghosts – at least not all the time. We are not lost in the narcotic stupor of bliss experienced in the god realms. And unlike animals, we have the capacity to question the reality of the 'trance' and to search for meaning in our experience and purpose in our lives. As humans, we have the right amount of favorable circumstances to make awakening *possible*, and the right amount of suffering to make us *desire* awakening in the first place. In terms of having the right conditions for following the path of awakening, the human realm is "just right."

But being human is not always a walk in the park. Even here in the Goldilocks zone, there exist horrors that are difficult to fathom for those of us who are privileged to live in relative comfort and safety. Many people were unlucky enough to be born in barbaric places where they are in constant danger of being bombed, raped or dismembered. The 20th and 21st centuries have provided many heartbreaking examples of human societies that devolved into living hell realms: a million Rwandans hacking each other to death with machetes; ethnic cleansing in Bosnia;

thousands dismembered by land mines in southeast Asia; the Holocaust of six million Jews in Europe; and, most recently, the horrors of war and waves of refugees fleeing from Syria. Closer to home, think of how many children grow up in abusive homes with barbaric parents who subject them to constant violence and threats. If you were born into a situation that is free from such horrors, you should appreciate how fortunate you are.

Some people, although they were lucky enough to be born in a relatively affluent and peaceful place, have minds distorted by ignorance and hearts hardened by prejudice. Ironically, it's often under the banner of fundamentalist religions that these spiritually immature people scapegoat and persecute their fellow humans. This is a tragic waste of a precious human birth.

You should count yourself as fortunate if you are free from such chains, and even more fortunate if you have unfettered access to spiritual practices such as meditation that help you tune into the better angels of your nature.

You have a human life and a human body, which is the most basic condition that enables your spiritual growth. Without this human body and its capacities, it would not even be possible for you to wake up. If you had the body of a horse or a dog or a cat, you could have all of the world's holy books in front of your face for your entire life, and not a single word of them would ever penetrate your understanding. The Buddha could stand next to you 24 hours a day and teach you about the path of awakening, and while you might very much enjoy his company, and even become close companions, the meaning of his words wouldn't necessarily penetrate your understanding. Think of how fortunate you are to be able to read and speak a human language.

Your ability to see and hear and speak and move about every day are things you probably take for granted – but these seemingly ordinary abilities are actually precious gifts that not everyone is lucky enough to enjoy. Imagine how

THE FOUR REMINDERS

much more challenging and restricted your path in life would be if any of these capacities were taken away. How often do you pause to appreciate the miracle of your vision, hearing, and other senses, or the things made possible by your fully functional legs, feet, and hands? These are among the faculties that made it possible for you to encounter this book about the Four Reminders and other spiritual teachings that guide you on the path of awakening.

The mere fact that you've encountered such teachings is a great gift in itself. For thousands of years, enlightened beings have been walking the path of awakening, and showing others how to do it. For every Neo, full of potential, there's a Morpheus who came along and offered him the red pill and opened his eyes to the greater reality outside the Matrix. Like Neo, your decision to keep your eyes open, to cast aside your illusions and do whatever it takes to see reality clearly, is the first step on the path of spiritual transformation. A much greater destiny awaits you once you decide to find out what lies beyond the Matrix.

The impulse to find out what lies beyond the Matrix might be the greatest gift of all, and if you feel that impulse, you are one of the few. So many people never even have the desire to wake up from the trance. Maybe the dreams they are having are too pleasant, and they would prefer to keep on dreaming. Maybe they started down the path of awakening, and then got sidetracked and gradually fell back asleep again. Or maybe they even started down the path and then backtracked because they realized that awakening would require them to do things that weren't comfortable, or to make decisions that weren't popular. If you have found the path to awakening and you also have the grit and determination to keep going, then you are as rare and gifted as Neo himself, who was also called The One.

Here Today, Gone Tomorrow

Part of what makes this human life so precious is its fragility and its fleeting nature. As we will see in the Second Reminder, a human lifetime is no more than a blip that flashes briefly on the screen – here one instant and gone the next. And even while you are here, you never really know when or how your circumstances might suddenly change for better or worse. Last year one of my acquaintances, a very athletic young man in the prime of his life, fell off a ladder while painting a house, and injured his spine. In a single instant, his life changed forever.

You may feel you are on top of the world today, but tomorrow you could be laid low by a virus or a broken heart, an economic calamity or a terrorist attack. You might be betrayed by friends or family, or by enemies, or by the government, or by your own body or mind. You are fortunate to live in this human realm, but the conditions that support your continued well-being are fragile, beset on every side by threats and obstacles. You never know when one of those threats might actually puncture the bubble and take all the air out of your inflated sense of security. Appreciating your human life and making the best use of it means never – not for one second – taking it for granted.

Ask yourself: how can I appreciate the gift of this human life and make it truly meaningful?

CONTEMPLATING THE FIRST REMINDER

Contemplation: Macro to Micro

Take a few moments to sit quietly and rest your attention on deep, calming breaths. Once your mind feels relaxed, contemplate the preciousness of your human life on both a 'macro' and a 'micro' scale.

First, on the 'macro' level, reflect on the good fortune of your life as a whole, and the positive circumstances and conditions that brought you into existence. Consider the beautiful, fragile world into which you were born, and the love and support you've received from so many people in your life to bring you to this moment.

Next, zoom in and focus on the past five years of your life. Take stock of all the things that have gone right for you in these five years, things you might ordinarily take for granted. Your heart has continued beating – nearly 200,000,000 times – without you ever having to think about it. You have been fed and clothed. You've probably been relatively free from violence and overwhelming fear. You've received spiritual guidance or teachings, and made connections with other, like-minded people. You've been

CONTEMPLATING THE FIRST REMINDER

supported and carried, and you've helped to carry others.

Now, zoom in even closer, into the 'micro' level: this year, this month, this week, today, this hour, and finally this very moment. Reflect on how many auspicious conditions must come together to make it possible for you to be sitting here right now, reflecting on your precious human life in light of the First Reminder. Appreciate the freedoms and positive circumstances that make this very moment of contemplation possible.

Now what are you going to do? What will you do in the *next* five-year phase of your life (if you're lucky enough to live that long)? What specific actions could you take – in this moment, this hour, this day, this month, this year – to make your human life as meaningful as possible?

Daily Practice: Say "Thank You"

There is a moment at the beginning of Wayne Dyer's film *The Shift*, in which he demonstrates how he would wake up each morning at around 3:30am. Rolling to the side of his bed, placing his feet on the floor, he lifts his gaze slightly, takes in a deep breath, pauses to appreciate the miracle of being alive, and whispers: "Thank you. Thank you. Thank you."

If you're like me, that's a far cry from how you typically wake up. You might utter phrases and perhaps even cry out to a higher power, but it's not in gratitude for another day of life. It might be more like: "Oh God! I hate getting up this early." "Oh God! I wish I didn't have to go to work today." "Oh God! I feel like a truck ran over me." "Oh God! My back aches / my head hurts / my allergies / etc…"

The writer Ben Okri once cautioned that you should pay careful attention to the stories you tell yourself. At night while you sleep, he said, "beneath the waters of consciousness," those stories are subtly changing your world. The same is equally true of the stories you tell

THE FOUR REMINDERS

yourself upon awakening, and all throughout the day.

What is the first story you tell yourself upon waking up, when you first open your eyes and set your feet on the floor? Is it a litany of complaints, a story about how much your day is going to suck? Then guess what? Your day is going to suck. You've pretty much willed that perception into existence. The stories you tell yourself are the lens coloring your experience.

What if you could wake up and tell yourself, instead, a quick little story about what a freaking marvel it is to be granted one more day of life? Imagine how it would change the narrative – and how the narrative would change your experience – if the first thing you articulate in your mind upon waking up is not a complaint about your day but an expression of gratitude for it.

When you come home at the end of the day and drop your bag and take off your shoes, notice the tone in which you exclaim: "Oh God! What a day!" Are you complaining about what dreary ordeal your day was? Or expressing wonder and appreciation for the fact that you were lucky enough to live another day?

Someday all too soon you will run out of days, and then you will see that, each day, the stories you told yourself about your life were, in fact, altering your world. You can't always change the circumstances of your life, but you can always change the story you tell yourself. So start now.

Say "Thank you." Say it three times, when you first wake up, before doing anything else. It doesn't matter who you say it to. Say it to your heart, for keeping you alive. Say it to your parents and your ancestors, whose dreams and hard work live on in your bones and in your blood. Say it to the morning sun and to the air that fills your lungs. Say it to the roof over your head. Say it to the great earth upon which you shuffle your tiny, insignificant feet. Say it to the small creatures, already awake before you, foraging or asking for their day's sustenance. Say it to the day that lies ahead of you, with all the blessings and challenges it may bring. This practice may feel phony or silly at first. You might feel like a new age Pollyanna. Do it anyway. And after practicing it for a while, see if it doesn't change your world for the better – even just a little.

•••••••

For additional suggestions on contemplating the First Reminder, refer to the accompanying Study and Discussion Guide, which you can download at:

www.thefourreminders.com

THE SECOND REMINDER

LIFE IS SHORT
(AND THEN YOU DIE).
DON'T WASTE TIME.

TIME IS NOT ON YOUR SIDE

The Buddha said that of all contemplations, contemplation of death is the greatest, just as the elephant's footprint is the greatest among all animals' footprints. This is because it is probably the most effective at shattering our false sense of self and undermining one of our greatest illusions: the illusion of immortality.

Of course, on an intellectual or rational level, you surely don't *think* that you are immortal. But on an emotional level, you go about your life as if you had all the time in the world – as if death were something that will of course happen to other people but probably not to *you*. You rarely give a thought to the incontrovertible reality of your own death, or to the complete uncertainty about the timing of your death. The Second Reminder is perhaps the most discomforting of all the Four Reminders, because it forces you to confront the painful and inconvenient truth that this precious human life you have is fragile and fleeting, and it will be over very soon.

In ancient times in India, Buddhist monks would go to charnel grounds to contemplate death in a very graphic way. Charnel grounds were like gruesome, open cemeteries where the corpses of the dead were left to decompose and be eaten by animals of prey. In some cases, they would even go to these horrific places at nighttime, in order to intensify the sense of fear they felt around the corpses and the nocturnal animals and perhaps even the evil spirits they believed haunted such places. The point was to look at death and its aftermath very directly, contemplate the actual decomposition of the human body, and come to the full realization that this is the fate that awaits you, me, and everyone else.

That's a far cry from the way we approach death these days. In 21st-century Western society, our habitual ways of relating to death are denial and avoidance. We prefer to think about death as little as possible; preferably not at all. To spend much time thinking about death, or relating to matters of death, is considered "morbid" or "weird" or "gross." We look askance at people whose professions require them to deal routinely with death and corpses. We wonder: how can they do what they do every day? How can they face it? We might even think there is something a little "off" about someone who would go into such a line of work. What could drive them to choose such a gruesome profession?

Our aversion towards death begins long before death actually arrives. As people grow old and infirm – gradually taking on more of the appearance of death and less of the appearance of life – we often tuck them away into nursing homes, into the care of people who are specially trained to deal with the challenges of elder care. Even half a century ago, this mass institutionalization of the process of aging and death would have been almost unthinkable. Elders were cared for at home, and death most often took place at home, as well. It was regarded as an unfortunate but natural part of the cycle of life.

Not anymore. Death today often takes place in clinical settings. It is regarded as a kind of systemic failure that occurs when medical interventions and science can no longer keep the body alive. When our loved ones die, we

THE FOUR REMINDERS

don't sit around with the corpse, the way people used to do. We hide it away in the morgue or the funeral parlor as quickly as possible. We turn it over to morticians who are specially trained to drain the body of blood, inject chemicals, and apply cosmetics to make the corpse look pretty and life-like and to keep it from smelling like an actual corpse. If any of us today were to stumble into one of the charnel grounds of ancient India, we couldn't handle the real sights and smells of death. We would probably lose consciousness immediately.

Perhaps you imagine that by not looking at death, by hiding all the evidence of it as much as possible, you can somehow escape being affected by it. If that's your approach, you are like the ostrich burying its head in the sand out of fear, imagining that by hiding its face, it is safe. But you can't hide forever. Sooner or later, slowly or suddenly, death will pull the rug out from under you. A beloved friend or family member may die, or an unwelcome glimpse of your own impending death may come into sight through illness or accident – and, suddenly, you act so surprised! *What is this? You're not immortal, after all?*

And yet, what could be more certain than the simple fact that you will die? There is something totally absurd about this human capacity to be surprised by the one thing – the only thing – in life that is *absolutely certain*. The simple truth is that all life ends in death, and through death new life is able to emerge.

When you are still relatively young, it is easy to take your life and your health for granted. You coddle and cherish your body, filling it with the best foods and dressing it in the finest clothes you can afford, taking great pride in looking a certain way. You might assume that your body will continue to serve you well, long into the future. But as you grow older, it becomes harder to remain in denial of the physical body's gradual slide towards decrepitude. Your body starts putting up resistance; it no longer

TIME IS NOT ON YOUR SIDE

cooperates fully with your wishes. You no longer look the way you used to look, and your body doesn't feel or move the way it used to; it is beset by mysterious aches and pains, and the common ailments that come with aging. The body no longer bounces back so quickly from illness or injury. At some dreaded and long-postponed moment, you come to feel that you have crossed "over the hill" and you are now coasting downhill towards the inevitable.

Looking at photographs of yourself as a child, it is easy to be reminded how quickly your life is passing by. I can remember being a child and looking at adults who were then around the same age as I am now, and thinking, "I'll never be *that* old." Even the idea of turning 40 years old was, to my childish mind, so absurdly, impossibly far off in the future, that I thought the day would surely never come. Now, the milestone of 40 has come and gone, and the decades that preceded it appear to have flown by like last night's dream. Where did all the time go?

Buddhist scriptures say that life is like a dew drop that evaporates in the morning sun; a bubble on the surface of the water that may pop and disappear at any moment; a bolt of lightning that streaks once across the sky and vanishes into space; a torrent of water that cannot be contained but rushes down a mountain side and is gone. Even under the very best of circumstances – if you are lucky enough to have a long and healthy life – *how long is that*, really? Eight or nine decades? Even a century goes by so quickly – and the older you get, the faster the sands of time seem to slip away.

I'm sorry to tell you, but the Rolling Stones lied. Time is *not* on your side. No, it's not.

NO ONE GETS OUT OF HERE ALIVE

Our ongoing avoidance of the unpleasant realities of death and impermanence is an essential part of the trance – part of what keeps us sleepwalking through life. We stumble through our days trying to stitch together a security blanket of pleasant experiences, and we like to pretend that our security blanket can keep us safe and warm, happily ever after. But "the continuous work of our life," wrote Montaigne, "is to build death." All the while, in the background, the time bomb of death continues ticking away, whether or not we ever notice or pay attention to its ticking.

Denial of death is one of the strongest and most common forms of psychological repression. We turn away from the unpleasant truth of death because we fear it; and we fear it because death itself is a vast mystery. We would prefer not to dwell on that mystery because we find the unknown deeply unsettling. Even if you believe in some sort of afterlife, you have to admit that you don't really *know* what lies beyond the opaque veil of death. Death is, and always has been, the greatest unknown. Like the event horizon of a black hole, no light or information crosses back over that threshold to tell us with any certainty what really lies on the other side. Some people believe that very specific things await us on the other side of that threshold; others believe that nothing at all does.

The Buddha taught that dwelling too much in speculative answers to this mystery isn't really very helpful. He said that it's like you've been shot with an arrow; you could spend your time trying to figure out what kind of wood the arrow is made of, where that wood comes from, who made the arrow, where the person who made the arrow came from; and so on. Or you could just pull out the arrow, removing the cause of suffering, and hope for the best.

Since you can't know for certain what lies beyond death's threshold, there isn't really much point in trying to figure it out. It's better to focus on living the best, most meaningful life you can, right now. But the Buddha also taught about the inescapable law of karma, which is the Third Reminder. What lies on the other side of that threshold, he said, depends a lot on the karma you accumulate here and now. From moment to moment, and life to life, karma rolls on like a cascading domino effect.

In Western iconography, death is personified as the Grim Reaper, carrying a scythe with which to cut people down when it's their time to go. His skeletal fingers protrude from his sleeves, and his cloak's great hood hides his face from view. He is the dreaded embodiment of the terrifying mystery that lies in wait for each of us. His visual representation causes shudders; his presence is unwanted; his movements inspire fear and evasive maneuvers.

But averting your eyes from death because it makes you feel squeamish or fearful in no way alters its inevitability – just as the ostrich that buries its head in the sand does not really escape danger just because the source of fear is hidden from view. It's simply a coping mechanism – and not a very good one.

From the time we are born, the candle is already burning from both ends; life is always getting shorter rather than longer. Advances in medical technology have brought many ways to temporarily prolong life. But these advances have done nothing to alter the basic human fear and aversion towards death; in fact, they might have made it worse.

We have become expert at keeping the body alive for longer and longer periods of time, even during times of extreme sickness. This has led the majority of our society – doctors and patients alike – to believe that with the right foods, the right drugs, the right surgeries, the right medical supervision, we could postpone the moment of death almost indefinitely. In the modern medical system, death, when it does come, is often regarded as a failure – something that could have been avoided if things had been somehow better managed. The last days of granny's stay in the hospice ward are scrutinized by lawyers for procedural mistakes that might have robbed her of a few precious extra moments, resulting in malpractice lawsuits for wrongful death that reinforce our culture of fear and uptightness around death and dying.

The Immortal Quest for Immortality

Humans have been dreaming of immortality since the dawn of time. Every culture's myths speak of some primordial quest for immortality: the Holy Grail, the Fountain of Youth, El Dorado, Shangri-La, and so on. Even our contemporary obsession with movies and TV shows about vampires, who live endlessly by feeding on the blood of others, is a dark mythological spin on this ancient theme of immortality.

The perennial human quest for immortality takes place today in university laboratories, carried out by white-coated scientists tinkering with human genetics and molecular biology in the hope of discovering the elusive key to stop aging and death in their tracks, once and for all. Instead of Shangri-La or the Holy Grail, today we place our faith in the miracles of science and medicine, or proper nutrition; but underneath, the story remains the same. We are still searching for the elusive, ultimate prize of immortality: a way to live forever.

We still keep hoping, against all odds, that the Grim Reaper has a weakness somewhere, an Achilles' heel that can be discovered and exploited to render him powerless over us. We still dream of finding the golden elixir that will banish death and dissolve the sinister spiderweb of aging and impermanence in which we are all ensnared. I know of a 'biohacker' who claims he will live to the age of 180 and plans to accomplish this mainly through his dietary regimen, which includes putting butter instead of milk in his morning coffee, along with a patented extract of coconut oil and other substances.

As part and parcel of this quest for immortality, we are obsessed with youth and its temporary beauty. We regard the natural and potentially graceful process of aging with almost as much fear and aversion as we regard death itself. We try to sweep aging and death under the rug so they don't need to be acknowledged. In the last hundred years, a multibillion-dollar industry has emerged with promises to erase or hide the evidence of impermanence and aging. We buy creams to smooth away wrinkles, and strip our skin with chemical peels; we inject our faces with biotoxins to freeze the muscles in place; we have surgery to stretch the skin taught again, or get implants that enhance our youthful and attractive appearance. With vacuums, we suction away the unwanted fat deposits that often come with aging. There is nothing inherently wrong with wanting to look and feel our best. But all we really accomplish with these maneuvers is a temporary boost in self-esteem and attractiveness. We cannot postpone the inevitable forever. Gravity always wins.

A handful of very wealthy people go so far as to have their bodies or their brains cryogenically frozen in perpetuity after they die, in hopes that some future leap forward in medical science will make it possible for them to be revived from the dead and to live again in a new body – perhaps even an identical body cloned from their previous one. Transplanted from one cloned body to another, with extra clones on backup to provide replacement parts in case of injury or organ failure, they imagine themselves achieving a kind of medically assisted immortality.

Old age, sickness and death are universal human experiences. It doesn't matter who you are, how good-looking or smart or athletic or powerful or rich or well-connected you are. As an old Italian proverb says, "Once the game is over, the king and the pawn go back into the same box." Sooner or later the time will come when you lose your mojo, and everything falls apart before your very eyes.

Death may come swiftly, taking you by complete surprise. Or it may come with agonizing slowness, so you see its form in the distance, creeping towards you and becoming more distinct day by excruciating day, yet still months or years away from actually arriving. But one way or another, it will arrive. And when it does arrive, you cannot bargain or buy or logically argue your way out of it.

The myth of immortality is just that: a myth. No one gets out of here alive.

The Uncertainty of Death's Timing

Although nothing could be more certain than the fact that you will die, at the same time you remain completely in the dark as to when your death will arrive, and in what manner. Sometimes death comes naturally at the end of a long life; other times it comes swiftly and unexpectedly, and all too soon.

You may die a peaceful and natural death at the end of a long life, leaving your loved ones to murmur expressions of gratitude that you exited this world after a good life and without too much suffering. Or you may die a sudden, violent, painful death, leaving your loved ones to gasp in horror and disbelief at death's viciousness, cruelty, and injustice. You cannot predict when or how death will come.

On an otherwise beautiful spring day in 2017, without warning, two of my friends and coworkers were killed in a shocking, horrific act of workplace gun violence. They were murdered by an employee who had recently been fired and was seeking vengeance. Their murderer then turned his gun upon himself and ended his own life.

I had just seen one of these colleagues a couple of hours earlier. She smiled at me and said hello, greeting me by name. Her friendly manner and warm smile brightened my morning. No one could have suspected that her life, and the lives of two other people, would be so brutally cut short that day. Even as I write these words, it's difficult to fathom this tragedy. It seems impossible and unreal.

We never suspect that death might lurk so close at hand, until it strikes suddenly and unexpectedly. Even if you are diagnosed with a terminal illness and a doctor gives you an estimate of how much longer you might expect to live, death may still come in an unexpected way. Doctors' estimates are notoriously fallible, and death might arrive much sooner or much later than predicted. Someone I knew who was diagnosed with cancer and emphysema lived for a decade with her condition, while my own mother passed away within a few months of her lung cancer diagnosis.

In November 2016, on the day after the U.S. Presidential election, a close friend of mine – a very strong young man, athletic and health-conscious – was suddenly diagnosed with Stage 4 brain cancer. After complaining of chronic headaches for several months, his doctor ordered imaging tests and discovered a seven-centimeter tumor sitting on his frontal cortex and extending into his sinus cavity. Because of the tumor's location, it was impossible to do a biopsy, so my friend was quickly scheduled for brain surgery to remove the tumor. He went into a high-risk 12-hour surgical procedure without any certainty that he would come out of it alive, or with all his faculties intact.

As it happened, the surgeons discovered once they got inside his skull that the tumor was completely benign. The Stage 4 cancer diagnosis had been a false alarm, based on imaging tests alone. They were able to remove his tumor completely, and he required no radiation or chemotherapy. The next day after having brain surgery, he went home. My friend's outcome was the happiest of surprises, after several weeks of fearing and preparing for the worst. But imagine how very different his outcome might have been, with only a slightly different twist in circumstances.

Despite all our advances in medical care and prolonging life, to be human remains an incredibly fragile, tenuous situation. Your body is like a bubble – a delicate sack of fluids and tissues propped up on a rickety frame of sticks – so easily ruptured, besieged from all sides by viruses and bacteria, harmful rays, and sharp objects. Your life might be here one moment and gone the next. The human body needs constant protection and support in order to avoid being snuffed out by a hostile world.

Death Lurks Everywhere

Although it may seem morbid to contemplate, you go through every day of your life surrounded by a thousand things that could cause your death.

A stroll through the city is taking your life in your hands, as you dodge speeding cars to cross the street and walk by sociopaths with guns hidden beneath their clothing. Even in the comfort and safety of your own home, you could be electrocuted in a freak accident or slip and break your skull open on the corner of a table. You could die in a sudden flash fire that rips through the neighborhood, or shake hands with someone and catch a flesh-eating virus. You could scrape yourself at the gym and be overtaken by sepsis, causing massive organ failure as your own blood becomes toxic to your body.

Death might already lurk unseen within your body at this very moment, preparing its attack in the form of a blood clot or a tumor not yet identified because it's too early to cause symptoms and draw attention to itself. An unforeseen natural disaster or terrorist attack might sweep away, in one deadly blow, the entire community in which you live. Or you might join the ranks of the roughly 400,000 Americans who, according to one study, die prematurely each year due to preventable medical errors.

Even your food, which you rely on to nourish and support your life every day, might turn against you and become the cause of death from listeria or botulism. In every gram of food you eat, you swallow approximately one million microbes. Some of those microbes are of the friendly sort, the ones you need in order to survive. Others are hostile and would kill you if they had the chance.

In fact, the regular defensive functioning of your immune system, from the time you were born, is the only thing that keeps the hostile microbes in your body from killing you. But even this defensive network could turn upon you, if you were to be struck with any one of several autoimmune disorders in which the body begins to attack itself.

If you were lucky enough to wake up this morning in good health, you should consider it nothing less than a miracle – or, rather, a lifelong series of miracles that has been unfolding, one after another, since long before you were born.

A traditional English version of the Second Reminder asks us to remember: "Death is real. It comes without warning. This body will be a corpse." It is very real, indeed, and it can and often does come without warning. But our socially conditioned denial and avoidance of the entire

THE FOUR REMINDERS

subject of death makes us forget this basic truth. Out of sight, out of mind. And so, when death brushes near, as it inevitably will, it always seems to take us by surprise.

TO LIVE AND DIE WITHOUT REGRET

Losing the fear of death starts with becoming more familiar with it, more aware of it – admitting that it will happen to you and that you have no idea when or how it will happen. Letting this inconvenient truth sink in – not just intellectually but at a deep emotional level – compels you to live your life with a greater sense of urgency. When you realize how little time you have left, even under the best of circumstances, you are less inclined to waste the precious time you do have.

Normally, you spend your life busily trying to fulfill your worldly desires and needs, imagining that this or that change in outer circumstances is going to finally bring you the stable and lasting happiness you seek. You keep grasping at the carrot dangling in front of you, and your grasping keeps you stumbling forward through life. Sometimes you fall, and get back up, and keep on stumbling forward. Sometimes you don't even have a clear vision of what you're stumbling towards.

If you're single, it's easy to believe that if you only had a boyfriend or girlfriend, a husband or wife, then life would be fantastic. Then, you imagine, you could really settle down and start living. But if you're married, it's easy to believe the opposite: if only you could *get away* from your husband or wife and be single again, then life would be fantastic. Or perhaps you don't seek fulfillment in relationships, but in your job and career ambitions, or in material possessions, nicer houses or apartments or cars or clothes. You might seek thrills by jumping out of airplanes or traveling to exotic destinations. In any case, the search for fulfillment in life is most often directed outwards, not inwards.

The Problem Is: You Think You Have Time

There's a quote attributed to the Buddha that is often shared on social media. Like many such quotes, it is probably not traceable to any of the Buddhist sutras; but it still rings true and sounds like something the Buddha *might* have said, which is why people keep sharing it.

"The problem is," the quote goes, "you think you have time." You go through life imagining that the future stretches out before you like a vast, endless horizon, and you behave accordingly. But when you look more closely, you realize you have no idea how much time is left in your life, and even in the best-case scenario, it's not really a lot.

Even if you suspect that life has a deeper dimension, and that you can wake up and escape from the Matrix, it's still common to think that there's no great urgency to the matter. Procrastination comes naturally. It's easy to put off until 'tomorrow' what you ought to do today. This is because you imagine that 'tomorrow' you will have more conducive circumstances. When you finally acquire such-and-such, or become this or that, or finish that never-ending series of projects – in some vaguely imagined future moment when you will at last have all your little ducks in a row – then, and only then, you'll be able to finally settle down and turn your attention to the important things. In some future moment, you imagine, it will be more convenient to set aside mundane concerns and focus on spiritual awakening. But for now, you have urgent, worldly business that needs your attention. Right?

When I lived in the monastery as a Buddhist monk, I worked in the office and received most of the monastery's written correspondence. It shocked me to see how many people sent letters saying that they hoped to come live at the monastery someday, when they reached retirement age and were done with their worldly responsibilities – as if becoming a monk or nun and retreating to the monastery were a viable retirement plan. The aspiration to get serious about their spiritual practice was a noble one – but they shared in the illusion that they could do so at some distant future moment when they would finally have all their ducks in a row. It was as if they imagined sliding into home base at the end of their lives and arriving at the monastery just in time to practice intensely for a few years and achieve some kind of enlightenment right before kicking the bucket.

Here's the problem with that line of thinking: what if you never get your ducks in a row? What if time runs out before that happens? Death can come without warning, at any time, in a thousand different ways. Walking down the street, scheming in your mind about how to get all those little ducks in a row, you might be struck by a bus. In an instant, all your precious ducks are wiped off the face of the earth and your life itself comes screeching to a full stop. This sort of thing happens to people every day, all over the world; what makes you think it couldn't possibly happen to you?

Here's another problem with that line of thinking: awakening doesn't magically get easier as you get older. In fact, the older you get, the more set in your ways you become; your habitual patterns become more hardened, more difficult to break. If you have found your way onto the path of awakening now, what are you waiting for? You're not getting any younger.

To Live and Die Without Regret

"My religion is to live and die without regret," said Milarepa, the legendary 11th-century yogi-saint of Tibet, who lived in Himalayan caves and practiced meditation constantly. What that meant, for Milarepa, was ruthlessly setting aside every mundane concern and focusing single-mindedly on spiritual awakening. After he attained awakening, Milarepa said that all his previous fears of death vanished once and for all. He went on to express his experience of awakened mind in the form of many "songs of realization" that are still sung today by Tibetan Buddhists, and studied as liturgical guides to meditation practice.

Unlike Milarepa, most of us fear death to some greater or lesser degree. Our *thanatophobia* – the technical term for the fear of death – is complex and personal. You might simply fear the unknown, and the possibility of nonexistence. Death is charged with mystery and uncertainty because you don't know what, if anything, happens on the other side of its threshold. Or you might not care much about what happens after death; you might fear the actual, gritty process of dying and the pain and suffering involved. You might fear losing control and dignity. You might fear leaving behind your loved ones and all your unfinished business.

Given how much we fear death and avoid the subject, it may be difficult to imagine dying with absolutely no trace of regret. For many people death comes by surprise, catching them completely unprepared and full of regrets. In death's cold light, they look back on the arc of their life story and agonize over things done or left undone, things said or left unsaid. They realize how many things they might have done differently, but there is no time left to change anything. The play is over, the characters have finished their lines, and the curtain is falling. Too often, death is a time of sorrow and remorse, a sad acknowledgement that one should have made better choices, or should have taken a different direction.

Imagine that, one hour from now, you were to suddenly find yourself lying on your deathbed, looking back over your life in your final moments. A lot of things that feel very significant to you right now would probably lose their significance. Things that used to hold great value for you in life might come to seem, in death's ominous shadow, utterly meaningless and trivial.

In her book *Top Five Regrets of the Dying*, the palliative care professional Bronnie Ware noted that the most common regret expressed by people approaching death is that they wished they hadn't worked so hard. They realized that they had spent too much of their lives running in circles on the hamster wheel of work and ambition, and, as a result, they felt like they never really got to appreciate life. They didn't prioritize things that were more important to them, like family and friends, because too much of their time and energy was consumed by work. And for what, in the end? Facing death, they realized that they would have to leave the fruits of their work behind, and all their unfinished projects would remain unfinished – forever. They couldn't take any of their work with them.

You Can't Take It with You

According to the Buddha, there is only one thing you carry with you when you cross that threshold into the great unknown of death. In the hidden reaches of your mind, you carry the accumulated seeds of your own karma – the impressions recorded in your mind-stream by your thoughts, words and actions during this life. (The chapter on the Third Reminder will look more closely at this idea of karma.)

Death terminates your personal narrative and brings an end to everything you habitually identify as "you" and "yours" – but death is not, according to the Buddha, the end of the whole story. It's just the end of "your" individual ego-story. When your life dissolves, the karmic seeds you planted in the world still remain, and will give rise to a new experience, a new narrative, a new dream – a new "you." Whether the next dream will be a pleasant one or a nightmare, the Buddha said, depends to some extent on what you do here and now.

In death, all your usual security blankets are stripped away; you cannot be saved by vast sums of money, or friends, or family; power and fame are useless; even your precious body betrays you as it becomes impossible to move, talk, eat, swallow a sip of water, or maintain control of your excretory functions. The one thing you *can* count on, the Buddha taught, is that the karmic seeds you carry in your mind as you cross death's doorstep will eventually come to fruition.

If you have planted dark seeds of anger, attachment and confusion, then those impressions will cloud and discolor your experience. But if you have planted seeds of compassion, love and wisdom, then those are the impressions that will arise and bloom. As Saint Francis of Assisi said, "Remember that when you leave this earth, you can take with you nothing you have received – only what you have given."

With time running out, and no certainty that you will not die sooner than you think, ask yourself: What karmic seeds are you planting? Are there blotches on your conscience that need cleaning up? What is really most important to you, and are you devoting your energy to that? What could you be doing now to ensure that your mind is not filled with regrets at the moment of death? What could you be doing differently – now, today, this week, this month, this year – to make your life more meaningful?

Why aren't you doing that?

THE GREAT LIBERATION

During the two years I lived in the monastery as a Buddhist monk, death seemed to be a recurring theme in my life. From my circle of friends and acquaintances outside, I received news of one loss after another. My friend John was horrifically stabbed to death in his apartment by his own lover. My friend Gregg, who suffered from depression and had tried to kill himself a few times before, finally succeeded in doing so. In the space of a few months, two other acquaintances died from drug overdoses. My grandmother passed away from old age while I was at the monastery, and Ani Palmo, one of the monastery's senior nuns, passed away in my presence. Even my own mother passed away the year after I gave up my robes and left the monastery. As I faced one human loss after another, I contemplated the frequency with which death was visiting my circle of loved ones.

It's true that death sometimes comes without warning, but at other times it mounts an all-out media blitz to warn people of its coming. It can arrive explosively, in a burst of unthinkable horror, as it did for my friend John and for my coworkers who were gunned down by one of their own colleagues. Other times, death sends word discreetly that it is planning to come at some point in the near future. Death can creep forward slowly over the course of many years, gradually tightening its grip with agonizing slowness, giving you plenty of time to think about it. That's how it came for Ani Palmo, who had battled first throat cancer and then emphysema for about a decade. She had rehearsed and anticipated and talked about her death for so many years that it became a sort of running joke at the monastery. Ani Palmo was dying, and she had been dying ever since most people could remember; but we wondered if she might end up outliving most of us.

I only got to know Ani Palmo during the last eighteen months of her life, but even then, with oxygen tubes in her nose, she was still a formidable character. As a young child, I was told, she had lived in Poland under Nazi occupation; after the war, she spent five years in an orphanage operated by nuns. A psychologist by profession, she left her first husband and two young children, remarried and emigrated to Canada in the 1970s. But she said she felt lost and confused amidst the drinking and drugging and sexual freedom of the era. After becoming a student of Tibetan Buddhism, she found her path: she divorced her second husband, took lifelong vows as a Buddhist nun, and eventually came to live and teach at the monastery.

Like an old-world Polish grandmother, Ani Palmo was famous for her hospitality, and for the cookies and chocolates and gossip she would offer to visitors at her cabin. But once you were relaxed and comfortable, she would turn her flashing, intimidating blue eyes on you and ask you – in her thick Polish accent – how your meditation practice was going. Her geniality was matched by her gravitas as a practitioner. Her students loved her passionately, and had a respect for her that bordered on fear – and for good reason. Despite her sweetness, Ani Palmo had sharp edges. She could be severe and demanding, and disarmingly perceptive.

By the time I knew her, Ani Palmo's health problems

had confined her to her cabin, tucked in the woods a short distance from the monastery, and she breathed with the aid of an oxygen machine.

I often drove into town – a one-hour drive from the monastery – and did the shopping for residents, so I was the one who brought Ani Palmo her supplies of cookies and chocolates. Her eyes always lit up when I walked into the room, and she would greet me with a cheerful "Hieeee!" or with my Tibetan monastic name, "Zöpa!" Occasionally, she would slip me a note asking me to bring her contraband, such as an "everything" bagel with garlic and onions (these are taboo substances for Buddhist monastics). We would share a conspiratorial smile: a woman who is actively dying is entitled to have the rules bent for her, just a little bit. Then she would invite me to sit down, offer me some of the goodies I had brought for her, and ask for the latest gossip from the monastery. She would often break down in a spell of acute coughing and wheezing, unable to catch her breath, the fluids in her lungs rattling in a guttural way that alarmed me every time I heard it.

With Ani Palmo there was none of the usual tip-toeing around the subject of death. It was constantly on her mind, and on her tongue. She anticipated death every day, and in fact she wished it would hurry up and come. It was long overdue, as far as she was concerned. Any casual conversation with her was likely to come around to the topic of her death, and she usually sent visitors away with some little cherished memento, in case they never met again: a photo, a tchotchke, a book about meditation. She seemed to have an endless supply of these objects, so her practice of giving them away was never finished.

Over and over, people who had known her for decades came to visit her and say their final, emotional farewells, knowing she would soon pass away – only to return in a year (or two or three) to find her still alive. At her 76th birthday celebration, she calmly told us that if her birthday

THE FOUR REMINDERS

wish came true, she would not live to see another birthday.

Like Milarepa, Ani Palmo did not seem to fear death much, or its aftermath. But what she did fear was the pain and suffering involved in the dying process. She had seen her mother dying, also from emphysema. She had experienced the horror of watching someone slowly drowning in their own internal fluids, so she knew the kind of physical suffering that awaited her. She was already deep in the grips of that suffering, and could only tolerate it with the help of strong painkillers and breathing treatments.

Yet, despite all that, she remained remarkably clear in her mind, and resigned to her situation. She had long ago accepted her illness as her own karma coming to fruition, and she did not resent it. Since, in her case, there was no possibility of looking away from death, she chose to fully embrace it. In keeping with the Tibetan tradition, she saw death as a great opportunity for liberation and awakening – but she also knew that, in order to seize that opportunity, one must rehearse, meditate, and be properly prepared for the moment when it comes. As the philosopher Montaigne said, "We do not know where death awaits us, so let us wait for it everywhere. To practice death is to practice freedom."

Tibetan Buddhists often take this advice quite literally. When I went to visit Ani Palmo I would frequently find her listening to a recording of *The Tibetan Book of the Dead*. This had been personally recorded for her, many years earlier, by Pema Chödrön, her fellow nun at the monastery. (Pema Chödrön, my teacher, is a well-known Buddhist author of numerous bestselling books on spirituality and meditation.)

The Tibetan Book of the Dead is a shamanic guide to dying as well as to liberation for the consciousness of the deceased person in what is called the *bardo* – the disembodied, in-between state after death but before rebirth. According to the text, this in-between state is fertile with the potential for complete awakening if the deceased person is trained to recognize the luminous, empty nature of mind and to rest in it with equipoise. Over the years Ani Palmo spent preparing for death, she must have listened to that recording of *The Tibetan Book of the Dead* hundreds of times.

During Ani Palmo's last stay at the hospital, about an hour's drive away from the monastery, we set up a team of people to take turns staying with her around the clock. On the day she passed, I went to the hospital for a late-morning shift. Serri, one of my fellow monks, was there along with Barbara, the monastery's executive director. Ani Palmo was unusually agitated, and tears were streaming down her cheeks. She was speaking fast in what seemed to be Polish, and struggling to catch her breath in-between phrases.

"Look, Ani Palmo," said Barbara. "Zöpa's here." Ani Palmo grew quiet for a moment and opened her eyes wide, taking in my presence as best as she could; I wasn't entirely sure if she still recognized me. Then her eyes relaxed again and she lapsed back into her Polish monologue. I sat by her bed for a while and stroked her hand and arm. Judging from the way she was speaking, it seemed she wanted desperately to communicate something, but we had no idea what she was saying.

Then, from somewhere within the stream of incoherent words, a few syllables jumped out at me, and I suddenly realized that Ani Palmo wasn't babbling incoherently, or speaking in Polish. She was reciting the familiar Sanskrit mantra of Padmasambhava: "Om Ah Hum Vajra Guru Padma Siddhi Hum." I began to sing the mantra with the melody we used for it in some of our practices. Barbara and Serri also knew the melody, and they joined in, so we formed a kind of bedside chorus singing in Sanskrit. Ani Palmo stopped speaking, her eyes still closed, and listened intently for a while as we sang the mantra, and finally she piped up again: "Om Ah Hum!" Those three sacred syllables from the mantra were her last clearly spoken words.

Ani Palmo raised her hand and gestured toward the portable music player that held her recording of *The Tibetan Book of the Dead*. Serri turned on the recording, and we listened to Pema Chödrön's voice as she began to guide Ani Palmo, according to centuries-old traditions, through the stages of the dying process and its immediate aftermath. Barbara and Serri returned to the monastery; their shift was over.

I was left alone in the hospital room with Ani Palmo and the vivid descriptions, wafting out from the little music player, of what one sees and experiences in the process of dying and in the *bardo of dharmata* – the moment when the consciousness of the now-deceased person reawakens as from a sleep, but no longer attached to its old physical body. In that in-between space, mind's innate, awakened clarity shines brilliantly and without obstruction – if only briefly – before it becomes clouded over again by old karmic patterns and the dreams of the subconscious mind. That brief moment of clarity is said to be charged with great potential for awakening, if one is able to recognize mind's luminous, empty nature and rest there, instead of drifting off into another dream.

The music player was set on repeat, and Ani Palmo and I listened to that forty-minute section of the recording two or three times before I began to understand that this was not just another rehearsal of death for Ani Palmo: this was the real thing. At a certain point her breathing abruptly changed and became strangely calm. I called in the nurse to look at her. The nurse checked her IV line and felt her forehead, then basically shrugged as if to say, "Who knows?" The nurse left the room, unfazed. But I knew. This was it.

I ran a washcloth under cool water and dabbed Ani Palmo's forehead with it. She was no longer responsive to touch, but I could tell she was still listening to Pema

THE GREAT LIBERATION

Chödrön's voice from the recording, and following the instructions in the text. Every once in a while she would respond to the recording with a non-verbal sound of recognition, just the smallest of grunts – but enough to tell me she was still there, still listening. Palliative care professionals know that hearing is usually the last of the senses to go, and often continues functioning even after patients no longer respond to touch or visual stimuli. The Tibetan Buddhist tradition, as well, says that hearing is the last of the senses to go; in fact, Tibetan Buddhists believe that hearing continues functioning even in the bardo, the in-between space after death, which is why *The Tibetan Book of the Dead* is read aloud both to people who are dying and to those who are recently deceased.

Gradually, the spaces between Ani Palmo's breaths became longer and longer. I began to silently count the time before her next in-breath: three seconds, five seconds, ten seconds, fifteen seconds. At some point I waited for the next breath and counted the seconds, and just kept counting: one minute, two minutes. I kept waiting, but she never breathed in again. In the end, after all those years of battling illness, Ani Palmo slipped across the threshold of death so peacefully that I couldn't even be sure of the exact moment when it happened. I reached out a hand to stroke her forehead and smooth her hair back, and whispered: "The struggle is over, Ani Palmo. You're free."

Death is the greatest uncertainty, and yet nothing could be more certain than the fact that we will die. We don't know when it will come, or how. And despite whatever we may believe and whatever tradition may tell us, we don't really know for certain what happens once we cross that threshold. But we can choose, to some degree, how we cross into the vast, open space of that mystery. We can go kicking and screaming with fear and regret, clutching in vain at our own reflection in the mirror that is shattering before our very eyes; or we can dissolve into the open space of the mystery, and trust that our small, limited reflection in the shattered mirror of self wasn't really who we were in the first place.

That morning, Ani Palmo became one of my greatest teachers. She taught me, by example, what the death of a great spiritual warrior looks like. To the last moment, to her last breath, her commitment to awakening never once faltered. Despite the complete deterioration of her body, the heavy medication she was on, and whatever traces of fear and anxiety she might have felt about the suffering of her physical body, she still maintained the clarity and strength of mind and the singularity of purpose to continue meditating right up to the threshold of death, and beyond.

CONTEMPLATING THE SECOND REMINDER

As mentioned earlier, the Buddha said that just as the footprint of the elephant is the greatest of all footprints, contemplating death and impermanence is the greatest of all contemplations – because it has the most potential to shake us out of the trance and make us realize the urgency of awakening here and now.

Each of the contemplations below may be practiced on its own, or in combination with one or two others. But don't try to work with too many contemplations in a single session. The topic of impermanence and death is by nature uncomfortable and somewhat provocative, because we are conditioned to avoid thinking about it. It may bring up feelings of resistance or fear.

Allow yourself time to sit and open to each contemplation and see what thoughts, memories, insights or emotions it brings up for you. If you find yourself feeling agitated in some way or putting up emotional resistance, be curious about your reactivity; it may be a clue calling your attention to something you should examine more closely. Be inquisitive about your experience. Don't rush.

First, sit for a few minutes and rest your mind on the breath, letting go of whatever distractions and extraneous thoughts may be occupying your mind. Then, read one of these contemplations and explore how it applies to your own experience. When you feel you are done with the contemplation, sit quietly for a few more minutes and allow whatever thoughts and feelings may have been stirred up to settle again. Let go and relax. Afterwards, you might want to note your thoughts and insights in a journal, so you can refer back to them later, and build upon your understanding.

Contemplation: Our Impermanent World

Reflect on the impermanence of the world in which we live. The earth itself, this tiny sphere which seems to us like the center of the universe, is a fragile ball of dust twirling through the cold and hostile reaches of space, assaulted by asteroids, blasted by intense solar radiation, and now ravaged by massive climate change that scientists agree is being caused by humans, contributing to a seventh mass extinction event that is unfolding before our eyes.

All the time, planets like ours, and whole solar systems, are coming into existence and being destroyed. Stars explode in supernovae, or implode to create black holes – in both cases destroying everything that lies within an almost inconceivably vast distance. Galaxies comprised of billions of stars, billions of solar systems, form and collide and are destroyed or changed into something else.

According to modern science, not even the universe itself is stable or permanent – it is expanding and losing energy, and some astrophysicists believe that it will eventually collapse back upon itself. Looking around at the universe in which we live, there is absolutely nothing we can point to – not a single atom – that has any permanence whatsoever. Everything is changing, all the time.

Now consider how this applies to you: to the cells of

your body, to the hopes and fears in your mind, to your material gains and losses. On the earth's scale of time, your whole life adds up to something that is almost too small to be detected. How can you take yourself and the little dramas of your life so seriously?

Contemplation: Life Is Like a Bubble

Whatever is born will die. Every sentient being is made up of impermanent causes and conditions: a body that is subject to aging and decay, sickness and death; a mind that is fickle and always changing. Imagine that at the moment you were born, somewhere an hourglass timer was turned upside down, and the sands of time began to slip inexorably away.

The blessing (or curse, depending on how you look at it) is that you cannot see that hourglass; so you have no idea how much sand remains in the top of the hourglass. Even if you still have most of the sand you started with, time is slipping away just the same, and will be gone sooner than you think. Once the timer starts, there is no pause or reset button. Reflect on the inevitability of your own death, and the deaths of everyone you know.

Contemplation: No One Gets Out of Here Alive

Consider the Italian proverb mentioned earlier: "Once the game is over, the king and the pawn go back into the same box." Reflect on the universal nature of death – the fact that no one who has been born can escape it. No amount of money, power, friends, family, drugs or surgeries can keep it at bay forever.

Has it fully sunk in yet that you too will die at some point? In the back of your mind, in some vague way that may not be fully conscious, do you imagine that you will be the first person in the history of the world to be granted a certificate of exemption from death?

Contemplation: Death Comes without Warning

The fact that death will come is absolutely certain – but how, when and where are completely unpredictable. Consider the possibility that you might die within the next year, the next month, the next week, tomorrow, or even later today. If you're lucky, death won't come so soon – but contemplate the fact that it could.

If death were to arrive without warning tomorrow, would you be prepared to go? If you were looking back on your life right now with the certain knowledge that you were about to die, would you feel regret over any of the choices you've made? Would your conscience be troubled by unfinished business or projects, or by unresolved conflicts with friends or enemies, or by things you did in the past that still haunt you? If death were upon you right now, would you be able to face it with the confidence that you had made the best possible use of your human life while you had the chance?

Contemplation: This Body Will Be a Corpse

Consider the impermanence of your own body. In your imagination, step outside your body and look at yourself now the way someone else might see you at this moment. Now imagine that, standing behind you, is your eighteen-year-old body; see yourself as you are now, and as you were then. And standing behind your eighteen-year-old body is your ten-year-old body, and behind that is your five-year-old body, and behind that is your body as a baby, just learning to stand up on two legs and take your first, hesitant steps. Behind that is you as a fetus, curled up in your mother's womb, and behind that – "you" only exist as two microscopic things, an unfertilized egg and a sperm cell, which have not yet fused together.

Somewhere behind that, "you" drop off the screen of existence; you are there only as potential. At this point, even the egg and the sperm cell that will eventually fuse together to spark the process of becoming "you" have not yet been created within your parents' bodies.

Stage by stage, go back in time in your imagination, and try to remember how it felt to inhabit your body in its earlier days. Do you remember was it like to be "you" when you were eighteen years old, or ten, or five? Look at your body's evolution over time, the amazing arc of growth and decay that brought you to be who you are in this moment. Now ask yourself: where is that arc leading?

You've looked at the former versions of yourself that stand behind you and led up to this moment – but what future versions of yourself do you imagine stand in front of you? What will become of your body from this point forward? Where is all of this headed?

Contemplation: Remembering Those Who Have Died

Consider all the people you have known who were once living and are now dead. You may have lost family members, loved ones, friends or acquaintances – or even people whom you considered to be enemies. Around the world, many people whom you do not even know die every single day – one person at a time, or in great numbers when disasters strike.

Since the time you were born, try to imagine how many people have died – including those towards whom you felt attachment, those towards whom you felt aversion, and those you didn't even know and towards whom you felt indifference. If you were to make a list of all the people who have died in your lifetime, how long would it be?

Contemplation: Loss of Control

Right now, you feel strong and capable. With little effort or thought, you can perform thousands of complex or simple actions – driving a car, cooking, eating a meal with your own hands and swallowing food without difficulty.

However, when death comes your capacity to do these things will diminish gradually or suddenly. The strength of your body will dissipate, until you can no longer stand or move about. You may not be capable of feeding yourself; you may lose control of your bowels and bladder. When death is very close, you may not even be able to swallow a drink of water.

Your mind, too, may undergo changes. You may not be able to think clearly; you may experience confusion, fear, even delusions or hallucinations. You might try to speak, but others may no longer understand your words or the logic behind them. Consider the helplessness and utter loss of control involved in dying.

Contemplate how this loss of control awaits you and every other living being.

Contemplation: Macro to Micro

Absolutely everything is impermanent and changing – from the Big Bang and our ever-expanding universe all the way down to the smallest subatomic particles, quarks, muons, and strings. Nothing stays the same even from one instant to the next. The largest creatures on Earth and the tiniest, single-cell organisms all are growing older, and all will die in one way or another.

Consider the many ways you've been affected by impermanence: how your body has grown and aged since you were born, and how your thoughts and emotions and opinions have changed. The things that occupy your time now are not the same things that occupied your time in earlier stages of your life. Relationships have come and gone, and perhaps friends have turned into enemies or vice versa. In your whole life, have you ever really experienced anything that was truly permanent?

Consider how different you were ten years ago, or even five years ago. You probably have a vague sense of a continuous "self" who existed then and exists now. But are you really the same? Where is that "you" who existed five or ten years ago? Look at your mind. It is a constantly shifting amalgam of thoughts and emotions, ideas and opinions, memories and fantasies, impulses and desires. Sit in meditation for 10 minutes and try to hold your attention on one thing, and observe how quickly and repeatedly it slips away to focus on something else. Where is the permanence in your mind?

Look at your body in this moment. You are a heap of elements that are constantly changing and moving. Zoom in closely, and look at yourself as if through a microscope. The cells of your body are constantly dying and being replaced with new cells. Now zoom in further: those very cells are made of atoms. Atoms, on their own extremely small scale, are made of vast reaches of empty space in which electrons circle the nucleus like entranced Sufi dancers. If you were to take a single hydrogen atom and enlarge its nucleus to be just one foot in diameter, its electron would orbit the nucleus from a distance of roughly ten miles. Every cell in your body is made of atoms like that, full of energy yet empty at the same time.

Zoom in even further: beyond the nucleus and its electrons, you find quarks, and beyond the quarks, strings and muons and diffuse fields of energy and chaotic potential that only a theoretical physicist can speak about intelligently. Nowhere in any of this can anything solid and permanent be found.

If nothing truly permanent, secure or reliable can be found in your thoughts and emotions, your body, your possessions, your relationships, or your world, the question remains: in what do you put your faith and trust?

Life passes by so quickly, even under the best of circumstances. Contemplate how important it is to make this brief life as meaningful as possible, while it lasts.

Contemplation: Will You Wake Up Tomorrow?

This last contemplation comes from my friend, the Buddhist monk Loden Nyima, and it's something you can try practicing on a daily basis.

Each night when you lie down to go to sleep, think: "Okay, this is it. This might have been my last day on earth. Now I'm going to sleep, and I might not wake up tomorrow."

This contemplation may sound scary. If it does, first, notice that fear, and be curious about what's behind it. Are you not prepared to die tonight without regret? Do you have a superstitious reluctance to even pretend that tonight is the night you will die?

Second, be very clear about the purpose of the contemplation: it's not that you're wishing to die tonight or anytime soon. Rather, the purpose of the contemplation is to get out of imagining death as some kind of hypothetical thing that may happen in the future, and imagine instead that it's something immediate: "Okay, maybe it's tonight. Maybe this is it. The exam is over, pencils down. Am I ready?"

•••••••

For additional suggestions on contemplating the Second Reminder, refer to the accompanying Study and Discussion Guide, which you can download at:

www.thefourreminders.com

THE THIRD REMINDER

**YOU CREATE YOUR OWN REALITY.
MAKE SURE IT'S A GOOD ONE.**

YOU CREATE YOUR OWN REALITY

"Karma," like "nirvana" and "samsara," is one of those ancient Sanskrit words that have entered the modern vernacular. Nirvana was the name of an era-defining "grunge" rock band from Seattle. Samsara was the name of a perfume, the epitome of seduction and desire. The word "karma" is often invoked on tip jars in coffee houses, in movies and music, and in everyday conversation. Most people have a basic idea of what it means, and they throw around the word "karma" rather loosely. Even the Christian Bible talks about the general idea of karma, characterized as reaping what you sow: "Don't be misled – you cannot mock the justice of God. You will always harvest what you plant." (*Galatians 6:7*).

If something bad happens to someone you don't like, or to someone who has done something wrong, you shake your head knowingly and say, "It's his karma catching up with him." He got what he deserved; he brought it upon himself. Or in a moment of *schadenfreude*, you say, "What goes around comes around," with a satisfied smirk on your face: your idea of justice has been served.

On the other hand, if disaster befalls seemingly innocent people, people you love, or people who haven't

YOU CREATE YOUR OWN REALITY

done anything obviously wrong – or if a 'bad' person is very successful – your trust in karma goes out the window, and you cry to the heavens: "Why?!" Your concept of justice has been violated, and you cannot see the purpose or pattern in such needless suffering.

In other words, you call it karma when it's convenient, when it syncs with your own view of how things are or should be.

Karma is often viewed as some kind of mystical force, a theistic power to 'believe' in, like the Fates of Greek mythology – the three white-robed goddesses who were believed to control the destiny of each person. But the principle of karma as the Buddha taught it is actually quite simple, and not particularly mystical. When you do something positive, it plants seeds of happiness and well-being; when you do something negative, it plants seeds of suffering. If you plant apple seeds, you get apples; if you plant pepper seeds, you get peppers. But the fact that we so often persist in planting pepper seeds while hoping to get apples illustrates just how misguided humans can be.

One of the literal meanings of karma is 'action.' When you act, it generates a reaction, an effect. Like dropping a stone in a pond, whatever you think, say or do generates ripples that radiate out through your mind and into the world around you. No action happens without a corresponding reaction. But there's no god up in the sky doling out justice and serving up these reactions; it's just how things work, like a natural law. Saying you "believe" in karma is like saying you believe that water is wet.

You don't have to look far to see how karma works. If you do something that violates your own conscience, motivated by selfishness or cruelty or avarice, then you experience negative repercussions within your own mind. For years afterwards, what you did still weighs on your conscience, and might come back to haunt you in the form of nightmares. It might even appear as external situations that you unconsciously manifest in order to replay the

THE FOUR REMINDERS

same karmic drama over and over again.

On the other hand, if you do something selfless, something that benefits others and brings more happiness and well-being into the world, then you experience positive repercussions within your own mind. You feel the resonance of the positive energy that you put into the world. You feel good, and your conscience is clear. This is a simple way to think about the operation of karma.

Sentient beings are creatures of habit – that is to say, creatures of karma. All the time, as we think, speak, and act, we create habits – propensities towards repeating the same kinds of thoughts, words and actions again in the future. With every repetition, it becomes easier and more natural to do the same thing again next time. On a biological level, you create neural pathways with your habits, like grooves in the circuitry of your brain that reinforce the habit's power over you.

Another way of saying this is that *you get good at what you practice*. If you practice aggression, delusion and greed, you strengthen those patterns. If you practice compassion, kindness and wisdom, you strengthen those patterns. In every moment, the patterns and habits you choose to strengthen determine, to a large degree, the quality of your experience in the next moment. That's another simple way to think about the operation of karma.

It's like you are always living in a movie. You might find yourself inside a horror film, a romantic comedy, or a drama with lots of shouting and tension. Your movie might even go back and forth between different genres, because you are making up this movie as you go along. But whatever kind of movie it is at the moment, you are like the hero or heroine, the producer, and the director – all rolled into one. Other characters come into your movie or leave it, and you become a character in their movies too. Your individual movie can even become entangled with theirs, so it starts to feel like you're both living in the same movie. In any case, much of what happens in your movie –

and how you react to it – is determined by the choices you make along the way.

The clearest way to translate the Sanskrit word karma is "cause and effect," or "effect and cause." Your experience in every moment is both the karmic *effect* of causes generated in the past, and the karmic *cause* of future experiences through the seeds you are planting right now. Whatever you practiced in the past is what you're good at now; and what you choose to practice now will be what you're good at in the future.

Another famous fake Buddha quote that gets circulated a lot on social media says: "If you want to know the past, look at your present. If you want to know the future, look at your present." It's unfortunate that this quote can't be traced to any Buddhist sutra, because it indeed sounds like something the Buddha might have said.

Let's say you have a five-year plan for your life. If your five-year plan is to become really, really good at suffering, and you want to win the trophy for Most Miserable Person Alive, then keep planting negative seeds and creating the conditions for more suffering. But if your five-year plan involves becoming better at freedom and awakening, and experiencing more love and compassion and peace in your life, then start planting those seeds now.

Micro and Macro

According to the Buddha, the same cause-and-effect principle that operates on a micro level in your everyday experience also works on a macro level by shaping and coloring your entire life. Like a tumbleweed, you are blown helplessly from lifetime to lifetime by the winds of your karma. Over the course of many lives you cycle through all of the realms with their different forms of bliss and suffering as various karmic seeds sprout and ripen into fruition. This is the endlessly turning wheel of life, the vicious circle called *samsara*.

THE FOUR REMINDERS

If the Buddha's idea of rebirth and multiple lifetimes is too much of a stretch for you, look at it metaphorically. You have had lifetimes within this lifetime; you have been many different people since you were born. There is a certain thread of continuity of awareness between my childhood self, and my teenage self, and my young adult self, and me today; but those four periods of my life feel to me, now, like they were different lifetimes, and it's difficult to see those four very different selves as the same person.

Whether you look at rebirth literally or metaphorically, the principle of karma is the same. The past shapes the present, and the present shapes the future. The present moment is a continual flux in which old karma comes to fruition as our present experience, while at the same time the seeds of future experience are being planted.

The real purpose and value of contemplating karma is not to try to explain your present circumstances, or to understand how you got to be where you are now. Rather, it's to exert a positive influence over where you go from here. Your fate is always, to some degree, in your own hands, and you continually shape the future by your present actions. You may be boxed in by societal forces or by personal circumstances in your life, but within the walls of your box – however large or small it may be – you always have the power to choose your actions. Will you water the seeds of further suffering and ignorance and attachment, and continue sleepwalking through your life? Or will you water the seeds of compassion, letting go, and awakening? Which habits will you strengthen? What sort of movie do you want to find yourself living in?

The Power of Intention

Often, what makes an action 'positive' or 'negative' – what gives it its karmic charge – is not necessarily the action itself, but the intention behind it.

Imagine that you're walking down the street, on a date

YOU CREATE YOUR OWN REALITY

with someone you really like, and you pass by a homeless man panhandling for money. Normally, you ignore homeless people, and you rarely stop to give them anything, because you are suspicious that they are con artists or addicts. But you know that your date volunteers in a soup kitchen, and feels strongly about helping the homeless. So this time, you stop to give ten dollars to the homeless man. Secretly, you're hoping that your date will be impressed by your display of generosity, and will see you as the sort of person who likes to give money to the homeless.

So is your action positive or negative? From the point of view of the homeless man, it doesn't really matter. It's nice that he's getting ten dollars, and he probably couldn't care less about your underlying motives. But you know what your real motives are, and you can't hide from yourself. You know it's not the purely selfless act you hope others perceive it to be.

Sometimes if you want to understand the karmic charge of an action, you can't look just at the act itself and judge it superficially as 'good' or 'bad.' You need to look more deeply at the intention and motives behind it.

THE BIG QUESTIONS

For thousands of years human beings have been asking themselves certain fundamental questions about the nature of our experience. How did I get here? Where am I going? Did I exist before I became who I am now? Why do I exist in this particular form, and not in some other? Why am I having the experiences I'm having? Why is there something rather than nothing? Why do good things happen to bad people, and vice versa?

These are big questions, and they sit at the heart of every form of religion and mythology that has arisen in human history. They fall within the branch of Western philosophy known as metaphysics, because their scope extends beyond (meta-) the purely material realm (-physics) to address larger, more intangible questions of 'how' and 'why.'

Buddhism is certainly no exception, and has much to say about the big questions. Tibetan Buddhism, in particular, has perhaps the most to say; it is the most mystical and metaphysical of all the schools of Buddhism. Historically, this is because Tibetan Buddhism was influenced by the shamanistic Bön religious tradition that was native to Tibet when Buddhism first arrived, as well as by the highly metaphysical Tantric Yoga and Vajrayana Buddhist traditions of India. Tibetan iconography is baroque with depictions of blissful deities and wrathful demons. Tibetan beliefs and practices related to death and dying include reading aloud a sort of travel guide to the afterlife for the benefit of a recently deceased person. And Buddhist explanations of the actual mechanical workings of karma are complex and thorough.

According to the Buddha, karma has something very particular to say about the big metaphysical questions. It offers a comprehensive explanation for how you got here, where you're going, why you exist in this form and not in some other, why there is something rather than nothing, why you have certain experiences and not others, why seemingly bad things happen to good people, and so on. Everything you experience arises as the play of your karma coming to fruition, intermingled with the individual and collective karma of everyone around you.

If you feel resistance to this idea or have trouble understanding how it might be the case, then start by asking yourself why. What other views do you hold that might conflict with the notion of karma?

There are two usual suspects, two philosophical frameworks, or styles of understanding the world and interpreting human experience, that tend to dominate our culture. On one end of the spectrum is what's known as theism or eternalism – which includes all the monotheistic and polytheistic religions with their thousands of gods. On the opposite end of the spectrum is materialism or nihilism, which encompasses the modern-day philosophy of scientific materialism.

Eternalism says that there is, inside each of us, some kind of eternally existing and essentially unchanging self or soul. Usually, eternalism goes hand-in-hand with theism, which says that someone else (you might call this someone else "God") is acting as puppet master and pulling the strings of your life. An outside, omnipotent power decides where and when you are born, what kind of body and life you will have, how long you will live, what kinds of experiences will happen to you along the way, and so on. When you die, this omnipotent higher power decides the destiny of your "soul," which is some sort of ethereal, essential and permanent version of who you are right now. Whether in heaven or in hell or somewhere else, this essential self or soul is believed to continue living after death, forever – that's why it's called eternalism.

The materialist or nihilist view, on the other hand, holds that there is no rhyme or reason at all to your existence here, aside from the brute laws of physics. Your life is a series of mechanistic events unfolding, somewhat randomly, in a chaotic existential vacuum. There is assumed to be nothing at all beyond the flesh and what we can perceive with our physical senses or with the aid of scientific instruments and mathematical theorems. When our bodies die, our whole being ceases to exist in any form whatsoever. Lights out, end of show. You can't even say there's a blackness or a void, because there's no one there to experience the void or the blackness.

Most people in our society tend to adopt one or the other of these two opposing but standard philosophical viewpoints, depending on family and social influences, and their own inclinations. It's common, in fact, to assume that these are the only viable options, and that you must adopt one or the other. You either believe in God (a.k.a. the puppet master) or you're an avowed atheist and materialist.

Failing either of those, the only other option most people see is to throw up their hands at the whole question and declare, "I don't know!" – or, more boldly, "It's not possible to know" – and therefore it is pointless to speculate. This is the *agnostic* approach,.

Together, these two diametrically opposed points of view – eternalism and nihilism – comprise our metaphysical heritage in the 21st century. Most of us were brought up to think about ourselves and the world in one of these two ways, or combining elements from both views. You may even have started out believing in one, only to later switch allegiance and start believing in the other. Religions are built around such beliefs, and wars are fought between nations and peoples in order to defend or impose one people's set of beliefs on another. Because these two views so completely dominate our society, it might not occur to you that there could be a third option, a view that lies somewhere in the middle, between these two extremes.

Karma: The Middle Way
Karma is the essence of that third option, the middle way taught by the Buddha. According to the law of karma, your experience and your existence are neither random and meaningless and purely material, nor are they dictated by a puppet master deity who pulls the strings from some hidden, ethereal location.

Rather, how you exist and what you experience are basically the fruition of what you have created for yourself. There is no eternal, unchanging self or soul; nor is there just an empty vacuum in which nothing happens. Your experience is vivid and perpetually unfolding, constantly changing, and it is not purely random; it is driven by natural laws of cause and effect. The way you experience the world is a reflection of your mind, and your mind is a reflection of the karma you've created. There is a constant feedback loop.

Sometimes your suffering or your happiness is very obviously self-created. When you say or do something, you might experience immediate feedback from the world. You say something hurtful, and it immediately comes back to bite you. In such cases the karmic loop is very short, and you clearly see the effects and repercussions of your actions. Because the connections are so obvious, you can learn easily from such experiences. At other times, though, something happens to you and you have no idea why. A stranger insults you verbally, seemingly without provocation, and you feel outraged. What did you do to deserve this? The connections between your experience and its possible karmic causes may be difficult or impossible to see.

But an inability to see a cause doesn't necessarily mean that it isn't there. An object quietly placed behind you does not cease to exist just because you can't see it. In such cases the karmic loop may be too long, and what you experience now may be the fruition of karmic seeds you planted so long ago that you don't even remember planting them. Other times there are simply too many factors at play, too many interwoven strands of cause and effect, so it's impossible to trace a specific effect to a specific cause. The whole thing seems confusing and unclear, and perhaps terribly unjust.

The Buddha taught that you have been planting karmic seeds or impressions in your mind for a very long time – not only in this lifetime, but for many lifetimes. Because of that, you have a very long backlog of unseen karma waiting to come to fruition when it meets with the proper conditions – like seeds that sprout when they are given the right soil, nutrients, water and sunlight.

According to this view, the constant unfolding of karma shapes your experience not only from moment to moment, day to day, and year to year, but also from one life to the next. Whether the timescale is small (moment to moment) or vast (lifetime to lifetime), it's the same basic principle of karma at work – just as universal physical forces such as electromagnetism are at work on the micro scale of subatomic particles and on the macro scale of planets and stars.

The Unreliability of Memory

Since our modern Western culture is steeped in scientific materialism and in Judaeo-Christian religious traditions, you may find the Buddha's talk of rebirth and multiple lifetimes difficult to swallow. Perhaps it even flagrantly contradicts your beliefs. Like any metaphysical concept, past and future lives are not something that can be measured in a laboratory or conclusively proven through research, and so they are regarded with skepticism – and rightly so. You might even scoff at the idea: if you've had all these supposed past lives, shouldn't you be able to remember a few of them? For that reason alone, many people dismiss the idea of rebirth.

But just for the sake of argument, think about the severe limitations of conscious memory. Do you remember what you had for lunch on the second Tuesday of last month? Surely a memory of that lunch was recorded and it must still exist somewhere in the unconscious mind, but you can't access it. Unless something special happened that day to make the lunch particularly memorable – or if you live according to a very rigid and predictable routine – it's very likely that you have no idea what you ate that day.

What about Tuesday of last week? Can you remember, with clarity, even that far back? Most people cannot. If you can't recall the details of something that happened only a week ago, it does beg the question: why would you expect to be able to remember things that happened before you were born?

The failure of memory to recall something is not, strictly speaking, proof that it didn't happen. Although you may not remember what you had for lunch last Tuesday, you probably *did* eat lunch that day. And whatever you ate for lunch that day became part of your human experience, and had a conditioning effect on your subsequent experience. As the truism goes, you are what you eat. The *result* of your embodied, human experience in this very moment, right now, was conditioned by the *cause* of what you ate for lunch last Tuesday, interwoven with countless other causes. The nutrients you absorbed during that meal, and the cellular and systemic functions fueled by those nutrients, continue to shape your experience even now.

If you were to say that there is no causal link between what you ate for lunch last Tuesday and the present moment simply because you have no recollection of what you ate — or if you were to go so far as to *deny* that you ate lunch that day because you can't *remember* it — you would obviously be mistaken.

Memory is extremely selective, tenuous, and unreliable. You've already forgotten the vast majority of your everyday experience in *this* lifetime. Because you forget so easily, this makes it possible to imagine that there is no causal link between past and present, and that your experiences just "happen" to you for no particular reason.

The Buddha taught that this is a deluded way of interpreting your experience. Things don't just happen for no reason at all. They also don't happen because of some imaginary puppet master in the sky, pulling the strings of your life. You yourself are the puppet and the one staging the puppet show. You may be blown about by the winds of circumstance, and of course not everything in your world is under your control, but to a large degree you hold your puppet strings in your own hands.

The Little Questions and the Big Questions

The principle of karma speaks to the little questions, like how your lunch last Tuesday affects your experience in the present moment. But it also speaks to the big questions: how you got here, why you exist in this particular body at this particular time and in this particular place, why you are having these particular experiences, and so on. At some point, surely you ask yourself the big questions. And you adopt some kind of philosophical position on them, even if it's just the agnostic stance of shrugging your shoulders and saying, "Who knows?" You have to figure out what view makes the most sense to you. You have to find our own personal truth.

Do you believe, for example, that your existence here – and, by extension, the existence of our universe, or the existence of anything at all – is just a random blip, something that happened by chance? Scientific materialists are happy to trace the origins of the universe back to an explanatory event like the Big Bang, and stop there – but why did the Big Bang happen and what was there before the Big Bang to cause it? Was there consciousness before the Big Bang? Do you believe that the body and the material world are all there is, and that mind and consciousness are mere by-products of the central nervous system? Does every aspect of mind die with the body?

Or do you believe, on the other hand, that there is some ghost in the machine, a soul that will live forever with essentially the same characteristics of personality, image, and identity that you currently possess?

If you reject the *eternalist* idea that you are a puppet who will live forever under the control of a great puppet master, and you also reject the *nihilist* idea that consciousness is a meaningless, random blip that came into being by accident and will vanish into permanent oblivion when your body dies – where does that leave you? If some subtle aspect of mind may go on beyond the death of the body, but there's no external deity controlling what happens to it – and it's not blown about haphazardly on the wind – then what?

What you are left with is the possibility that the mind and its experiences are shaped by a force or principle that is inherent to the mind itself. There isn't anyone else running the show – you're running the show, and starring in it, and watching it, and believing all too much in the reality of the story you're telling yourself. That's karma.

The constantly unfolding cycle of birth, life, death and rebirth is happening in every moment. The Buddha called this cycle *samsara*, and it is depicted in ancient texts as a turning wheel with its six realms. When you remain ignorant of how you create karma, you go in circles on that wheel and generate a lot of unnecessary suffering and pain for yourself and others. You find yourself caught again and again in the same sticky situations, unaware of how you got there or how to get out.

The Good and Bad News About Karma

As the Second Reminder points out, when death comes you will be helpless. You will lose everything that you've ever clung to in your life. You will be unable to stop death itself, no matter how much you might want to turn it back. And you are unable to know for certain what might become of you once you go beyond the event horizon into the darkness and mystery of death itself. Whatever your personal belief system says about an afterlife or the lack thereof, you have to admit that *you don't really know for sure* — and not knowing makes you feel even more helpless.

The Third Reminder adds another nuance: when death comes and you lose control over this life, your karma will shape what happens next. At death, your whole internal and external world of body and mind falls away. You lose all the reference points you've ever had for understanding who you are and managing your experience. At that point of total loss of control, you are helplessly driven forward by the force of the karma you've accumulated and the conditions with which you meet. According to the Buddha, the stream of your karmic impressions and habits that has been driving your experience all along will arise again in some new shape, and the unending cycle of birth and death and rebirth will continue.

Tibetan Buddhists believe that those with a high degree of realization and awakening are capable of directing this process of rebirth consciously, or even choosing to abstain from it. But for the ordinary beings like you and me, enslaved by our karma, the whole affair is rather choiceless. We are helpless to stop it or control it. By the time death comes, it will be too late to change the balance of positive and negative karmic seeds in the mind, and you won't have the power to decide which seeds will sprout and grow into your next moment (or next lifetime) of experience. Because you lack awareness and control over your own mind, the whole samsaric process is a crap shoot.

Think about it: even at this moment, how much control do you have over where your mind goes, what it settles on, and how long it stays there? If you have any experience at all with meditation, you know what the answer is: not much! The human mind is as restless and unstable as a flea, hopping from one thought to the next, to the next, to the next. Your mind flip-flops between being agitated and being spaced out, and you fall prey to emotional storms of lust and anger and numbness. Vast portions of your mind are hidden from your conscious view in the subconscious storehouse of memories; things stored there sometimes bubble to the surface, triggered by associations or seemingly at random. Haunted by your past and goaded into fantasies about the future, you actually spend surprisingly little time just being here in the present moment, paying attention to your real, lived experience as it's happening.

How much control do you have over your mind? How long can you consciously direct your attention to one thing and hold it there without distraction? One minute? Thirty seconds? Ten seconds? Five seconds? How long before you realize that your mind has wandered and you've been carried off into another train of thought?

And that's not even the scary part. Right now your restless, agitated mind is relatively comfortable and secure. Imagine how your mind will react at the time of death, when all familiar reference points dissolve, when comfort and security are ripped away and you are left facing – alone and without protection – the ultimate discomfort and insecurity of dying. Do you imagine you will suddenly, miraculously have greater control over your mind at that final, crucial moment? Will you be able to rest without fear or distraction in whatever arises, and see its empty nature? Will you be able to consciously shape what happens next?

There are a few prominent skeptics among Buddhist teachers in the West, who say that karma and rebirth are merely antiquated superstitions: soothing promises of an afterlife designed to console those who are not mature enough to face the actual finality of death. One popular teacher who calls himself a 'Buddhist atheist' argues that ideas of karma and rebirth should be jettisoned from contemporary Buddhism altogether. He says that such ideas are not only unproven (and perhaps unprovable) but they offer false comforts and consolations, and they come dangerously close to proposing the idea of an eternal soul that migrates from life to life. The Buddha was quite clear in his teachings that there is no soul (no 'Atman' in the Sanskrit language of ancient Indian philosophical systems), no self that exists in an independent, permanent, and singular way.

But what these diehard skeptics fail to see is that there is nothing consoling whatsoever about the cycle of rebirth the Buddha described: it is, on the whole, a horror show of unimaginable proportions. And more to the point, there is nothing personally comforting to you as an individual about the prospect of rebirth, because here's the big let-down: it won't be 'you' who is reborn. It will be, quite literally, someone else. There is no individual soul that flies around from body to body carrying your personality and your image and the know-ledge of your taste in music and your favorite cookies.

When you die, everything you ordinarily think of as 'you' vanishes, forever. "Gone, gone, gone beyond, gone completely beyond," as a famous mantra from the *Heart Sutra* says. Your name, your identity, your history, your thoughts and memories, your relationships, your wealth and possessions, your accomplishments, your hopes and dreams – all of that disappears. Only karmic seeds remain, planted deep in a substratum of the mind that precedes consciousness, and some of those seeds planted there will sprout into something new.

A perplexed student once asked the Tibetan meditation master Chögyam Trungpa to explain: if there is no Atman or personal soul that transmigrates from body to body, what is it that gets reborn? Trungpa replied in his characteristically blunt way: "Your bad habits."

When death comes it will be too late to start planting better karmic seeds. What's done is done. The test is over. Pencils down. Helpless, stripped of your defenses, with all your future plans and schemes tossed out the window, you'll be out of time and out of luck. At that point, whatever comes next will be beyond your control. That's the bad news.

The good news is that *right now* – in this moment and every moment – you have the power to work with your present circumstances and lay the groundwork for a better future. You can start creating the causes for happiness and freedom right now, no matter where you are or what you're doing, and you can stop creating the causes for further suffering. Don't settle for a wait-and-see attitude, hoping that life and death will work out for the best. And don't sit around waiting for some external savior to swoop in at the last moment, redeem you from your suffering, and shower you with everlasting happiness, because that isn't going to happen. Stand up and take responsibility for yourself. Start now.

No Person Is an Island

Your individual experience does not happen in a vacuum. We are social creatures, enmeshed in a matrix in which our actions affect other beings and their actions affect us.

THE FOUR REMINDERS

When the hippies of the 1960s talked about good and bad 'vibes' and the ways we affect each other with our vibes, they were on to something. When you suffer, you tend to make others suffer with you; and when you are happy, you tend to make others happy too. But the same principle works in reverse. When you regard the suffering of others through eyes of compassion and do what you can to help, it lessens *your* suffering too; and when you make others happy, you yourself become happier as a result. Your personal karma intermingles with that of the people around you, until it becomes challenging to locate the edges between the personal and the collective. We are all swimming in this soup together, and we affect each other with everything we say and do.

Even without saying or doing anything, you can affect other beings simply through the energy you bring, the state of mind that you manifest in their presence. If others can sense your tension and aggression, it affects them negatively on an emotional level; by contrast, if they can sense your love and compassion and relaxation, it affects their emotional state positively. Just by the way you look at someone – a brief glance cast at a passing stranger in the subway or on a sidewalk – you can alter the tone of someone's entire day and have an impact on their life that you cannot know and could scarcely imagine. This, too, is part of the web of karma in which we are all embedded.

The more you contemplate karma, the more it hits home that everything you do, say, or think matters. Nothing you do is without consequences. At times, you might like to imagine that you can do something that goes against your own conscience, and get away with it; you tell yourself there won't be any ramifications, as long as you don't get caught. But this bubble is popped when you begin to understand how your mind and your experience of the world are permeated by the cause-and-effect principle of karma. Every moment of being alive and awake as a human being on planet earth has ethical implications, because even the thoughts and intentions that go through your mind have the power to generate positive or negative effects – and therefore to create happiness or suffering.

The human mind is somewhat myopic. Usually, you can't see very far beyond your immediate surroundings and the two or three layers of causes and effects nearest to you. But the web of interdependent causes and conditions in which you exist is immensely vast, and complex beyond your imagination. The *Avatamsaka Sutra* describes the metaphor of Indra's net, a web of infinite dimensions with a multifaceted jewel at each node, reflecting all the other jewels in the net, infinitely. Each of us is one of those jewels, interconnected and reflecting one another *ad infinitum*.

You cannot truly differentiate a piece of paper from the tree and the soil and the sunlight and the rain that produced it. The same is true of you and every other being; we exist in total interdependence upon our world and upon each other. Without the explosion of distant stars and the formation of galaxies and planets and solar systems, the very earth upon which you and the piece of paper briefly exist and cross paths would never have come into being.

According to the Buddha, this realm in which we live – the human realm, our fragile home planet, the universe itself – is all arising through the collective karma of the beings that inhabit it. We're in this thing together.

PLANTING SEEDS IN THE GARDEN OF GOOD AND EVIL

The words "good" and "evil" are blunt and problematic. They lack nuance and sound slightly antiquated, like throwbacks to an earlier time – perhaps Victorian England, or 1950s America – when society held more simplistic, black-and-white ideas of morality. When you hear someone talk about "good and evil" you might picture a stern-faced nun wagging her finger at you, reminding you to be a good boy or girl or face punishment.

But karma is not like a judge, doling out punishments and rewards for following or breaking the rules. It's not as theistic as all that. Karma doesn't "judge" what you do because it's not an entity – it's simply a description of how the minds of sentient beings work. Just as water is always wet, fire is always hot, and planets and stars always have gravity, your mind is always in the flux of karmic cause and effect, always hovering at the juncture between in-folded causes and un-folding effects. You don't always have a choice about which of your karmic seeds will come to fruition at any given moment – but you do have a choice about how you respond. And based on that response, karma continues to snowball: whatever direction you roll it in, it accumulates more mass, and more momentum.

At any point, you can roll the snowball in the direction that leads to more suffering and imprisonment and sleep, more aggression and jealousy and greed and ignorance, or you can roll it in the direction that leads to more freedom and awakening, more compassion and loving-kindness and peace of mind. In every moment, you have a choice, and the choices you make come back to haunt you (or delight you) as the fruit of your own experience. Karma may sometimes seem complex and unfathomable, but at heart it's really very simple. If you plant lemon seeds, you don't get apple trees. You get lemon trees.

Even a creature like Frankenstein could understand karma. *Creating suffering bad. Creating happiness good.* It's not rocket science.

There is no Big Daddy in the sky who's watching and judging your actions and deciding on punishments and rewards. Big Daddy is you: it's your own mind. The reason karma is so infallible is because there's no way to escape or hide from your own mind. You don't need a prophet coming down the mountain with a set of tablets inscribed with commandments from Big Daddy to tell you what is right and wrong. You already know. When you do something selfish, aggressive or greedy, you have built-in feedback mechanisms in your own mind that tell you so. When you do something that violates your own conscience, you suffer because of it, one way or another. You can't hide from karma because it's not out there coming for you – it's already inside you.

Without some kind of ethical compass, your life becomes a mess – and you become haunted by the mess. You harm yourself and others with your thoughts, words and actions, and the consequences of this behavior torment your mind and body. If the apple is rotting from the inside, no amount of polishing its surface will make it edible. Cultivating ethical behavior is what makes the apple wholesome, from the inside out.

Unfortunately, the still, small voice of your conscience is sometimes nearly inaudible, and your actions don't always reflect your deepest values. At certain moments you temporarily forget what your values are, or prioritize something else that seems more important at the time. Perhaps you tie yourself up in knots of self-justification and denial in an attempt to rationalize actions that don't harmonize with your values. Or, faced with temptation or challenging circumstances, you just get confused about what is the right thing to do. Losing sight of your ethical compass, you get yourself into trouble – and, from a karmic point of view, plant more negative seeds. And so the wheel keeps turning.

Ethics in Yoga and Meditation

Over the past couple of decades, yoga has taken Western society by storm. Beginning with a few transplanted Indian teachers and their ashrams, countless styles and schools of yoga have evolved to address every niche market and demographic: hot yoga; bootcamp-style power vinyasa; yoga for sexy glutes and abs; devotional yoga done in white clothing, complete with chanting, harmoniums, incense, and murals or statues of Hindu deities; corporate yoga done in front of computer screens or at office desks, wearing suits and dress socks; yoga for children; yoga for the elderly; yoga for obesity; yoga for women; yoga for men; prenatal yoga; postnatal yoga; alignment-based yoga; Christian yoga; dance-based yoga; Pilates-based yoga; yoga for sleep; yoga for sex; martial arts-based yoga; acro-yoga; partner yoga; aerial yoga; and, yes, even hot nude yoga.

More recently, there has been a similar growth wave of interest in meditation. Starting with a few Buddhist meditation centers established by teachers from Asia, meditation has grown into a cottage industry, and "mindfulness" is now a household word in mainstream society. Mindfulness courses are taught in corporations to help employees be less stressed out and more productive; in hospitals to help patients cope with pain and illness; in classrooms to help students concentrate and perform better on tests; in church basements to help addicts in recovery; in therapists' offices to help patients regulate mood disorders; in temples to help spiritual aspirants reach towards enlightenment; in boutique secular meditation centers to help busy urban professionals find time to slow down and relax; in the military to help soldiers cope with the acute stress of warfare.

With yoga and meditation quickly finding their way into so many corners of Western society, and taking on so many new – and often materialistic – manifestations, it's worth taking a step back to ask whether something essential is being lost in the translation of these ancient Eastern traditions into modern culture. What's being lost, unfortunately, is a focus on ethics and karma. Just like the apple that rots from the inside, polishing yourself with yoga or meditation is pointless if your behavior is not in alignment with your ethical values.

The famous second line of the *Yoga Sutras of Patanjali* says: "Yogas citta vritti nirodah," which roughly translates as, "Yoga is the quieting of the mind's agitation." But the mind's agitation is the result of karmic patterns and traces that linger there. So it all comes back to karma.

Picture a three-legged stool. The stool doesn't stand up on one leg, or even two. It needs all three legs to remain upright and be functional. The way the Buddha taught meditation (*Samadhi* in Sanskrit) was part of a whole package, a way of living that aligns every aspect of your life to point in the direction of awakening. Meditation, as the Buddha taught it, was never intended to be divorced from the other two legs of the stool, which are ethics (*Sila*) and wisdom (*Prajna*).

Traditionally, ethics comes first. You start by getting your everyday conduct and relationships in order, aligned

THE FOUR REMINDERS

with basic ethical principles, so that your life naturally becomes more workable and your mind becomes more clear (karma!). From that foundation of ethical clarity, it becomes easier to cultivate deeper wisdom and insight, and you carry that wisdom and insight into your meditation practice, where it all comes to full ripening (karma again!).

The same holds true in yoga. In the famous 'Eight Limbs of Yoga' described by Patanjali, there is a logical sequence. The first two limbs of yoga are about putting your life in order through the practice of the *Yamas* and *Niyamas*, yoga's ethical guidelines. It's only when you get to the third of the eight limbs, *Asana*, that you embark on the physical practice of putting the body into the familiar poses we think of when we talk about 'yoga.' When your actions, speech and thoughts are aligned with fundamental ethical principles, then the physical practice of yoga has transformative potential. But stripped of its ethical context, yoga is just a fitness routine, a series of stretches and fancy gymnastic tricks that a chimpanzee could be trained to perform far better than you ever could.

A building is only as solid and stable as its foundation. Lay a strong ethical foundation for your spiritual practices – yoga, meditation, prayer, and so on – and they can have transformative power. But fail to lay a proper foundation, and sooner or later the building will collapse.

Ten Things to Avoid

The Buddha taught about ten negative actions that – generally speaking – create bad karma and keep us stuck in the cycle of self-created suffering. The mere fact that there are ten of these actions may remind us of another famous list of actions to be avoided – the Ten Commandments. But the ten negative actions described by the Buddha are not a set of commandments, and the Buddha is not an authority figure with the power to command us or tell us what to do. Rather, these are guidelines or suggestions to help us work more skillfully with our own karma. The Buddha didn't speak in terms of moral absolutes; remember, to understand karma you need to look not only at the action itself but also at the intention behind it.

These ten actions are best avoided because – with rare exceptions – they tend to generate negative karma, rolling the snowball in the direction of creating further suffering and harm. 'Harm' is the operative word here. The Buddha's definition of an action that is negative or unethical or 'evil' is one that creates harm (*himsa* in Sanskrit). The ethical system taught by the Buddha is based not on some absolute principle of right and wrong, but on the simple goal of non-harming (*ahimsa*). The same is true of yoga.

The ten negative actions are grouped into three categories: physical, verbal and mental actions.

Three Physical Actions

The first and most obviously harmful negative action we can commit physically is *killing*. Killing means intentionally causing the death of another being. No living being wants to be killed; all creatures instinctively fear death and the suffering involved in it. Even a fly fears the hand that moves toward it suddenly, and attempts to fly away.

The second negative action is *stealing*. When we take what is not offered, we harm others by depriving them of what rightfully belongs to them. This can include stealing openly (by force or intimidation); stealing in secret (by stealth or burglary); or stealing through subterfuge, trickery or deception.

These days, in the business world, many people are proud and satisfied when they are able to succeed by trickery, swindling other people into handing over their money. And the opportunities today for perpetrating such deceit and theft on a massive scale are unprecedented. Our global economy and monetary instruments – hedge funds, derivatives, options, and futures – have become complex and difficult to understand even for highly skilled financial experts. The possibilities for trickery and deception, and the scope of this deception's impact on people's lives across the planet, have been multiplied exponentially.

Only a few years ago, the economies of the United States and most of the world's industrial nations were devastated by a systemic financial collapse that was created through rampant, institutionalized practices of deceit and corruption. The plague of toxic mortgages and securities, and the resulting collapse, crippled the global economy and drove numerous corporations and investors to bankruptcy.

In the simplistic barter economy of old Tibet, yak herders and barley farmers may not have known anything about toxic mortgages and options trading, but they were quite familiar with the motivations behind our modern-day economic calamities. Greed, trickery and stealing through deception may be practiced today on a scale that was previously unimaginable – and the suffering and harm caused by them can be more far-reaching than ever before – but they are nothing new. Cheating a fellow farmer on the price of a cow and cheating one's fellow citizens through corrupt investment practices both stem from the same motivation: hoping to make a quick profit at someone else's expense, and without getting caught.

The third negative physical action is *sexual misconduct*. Our human sexual energy wields a powerful influence over us and over those with whom we choose to share it. When we misuse this energy, indulging it in ways that are selfish or abusive or addictive, we harm ourselves and others.

Defining what qualifies as "sexual misconduct," however, can be a bit tricky. By comparison, the previous two negative actions are pretty simple. Killing is killing, and stealing is stealing. What was considered killing or stealing in old Tibet, a thousand years ago, is still considered killing or stealing today in modern Western societies. But what is considered appropriate and inappropriate sexual behavior changes with time and culture.

Certain sexual acts are universally taboo, and have remained so throughout history. Rape, adultery, child molestation and human trafficking are, by and large, frowned upon and criminalized in almost every culture. Few people would raise their hands to vote in favor of such things.

But when it comes to other sexual behaviors whose moral codes are not so black-and-white, society's views of what is appropriate and acceptable evolve over time. Changing attitudes and laws regarding homosexuality, same-sex marriage, and so on, are examples of this.

Sexual misconduct is simply any sexual act that causes harm. When partners commit adultery and cheat on each other, someone gets hurt. When someone forces another person to have sex against their will, the victim's dignity and the sanctity of their human body are violated. When someone has sex with a child, the child's innocence and trust are violated, and the emotional damage can follow the child into adulthood. These things are quite obviously sexual misconduct – and they obviously plant negative karmic seeds in the mind.

But elsewhere, the lines are not so clearly drawn. Among consenting adults who are not harming one another, and who are not committed to another person, it's largely assumed that they can decide for themselves what is appropriate sexual behavior. You cannot say that a particular sex act is right or wrong simply because of gender, sexual orientation, or the bodily appendages or orifices involved. To look towards a priest or a celibate monk – or a holy book written thousands of years ago in a primitive and feudal society – to tell you how you should or should not be allowed to have sex is to infantilize yourself and surrender your autonomy to ancient moral codes that have outlasted their usefulness.

Casual sex is a gray zone. In days gone by, excessive promiscuity was strictly defined as anything that happened outside the context of marriage. But in some social circles today, casual sex is celebrated, for better or worse. We are living in the age of booty calls, friends-with-benefits, and smartphone hookup apps that can geo-locate the nearest potential sex partner matching your specified criteria. Films and TV shows and magazines and the Internet bombard us with depictions of casual sex as a lifestyle. In this social context, finding the line separating casual sex from excessive promiscuity is not always easy. The choice may be a very individual and personal one. No one else can tell you what is right for you in these matters; only you can decide that. (Fifty shades of grey, indeed.)

Practicing right sexual conduct means asking yourself: Is it skillful? Does what I'm doing harm me or harm someone else? Recognizing how powerful sexual energy is, am I using it wisely? What are the psychological, emotional and physical effects of my behavior? How do my actions affect my partners? Am I sensitive to their feelings as well as my own? And how do their actions affect me? What sort of karma are we co-creating together through our sexual behavior?

Four Verbal Actions

Because so much of human interaction involves speaking and listening to one another, speech is another area of our lives where we have tremendous potential for creating positive or negative karma.

The first negative verbal action is *lying*. When you say something false in order to deceive others for your own benefit, you betray their trust. But there are also lies of omission, when you remain silent about an important truth that really ought to be spoken.

The second negative verbal action is *sowing discord*, or *divisive speech*. This can take many forms: character assassination, malicious gossip, and so on. You can openly sow discord between two people by turning them against each other, or do it secretly and furtively by talking about someone behind their back.

The third negative verbal action is *harsh speech*. This means insulting someone to their face, or making rude remarks about them to another person. Harsh speech is any kind of offensive speech that would make someone unhappy or uncomfortable if they heard you saying it. Sometimes harsh speech may be couched in a nice tone of voice or hidden behind a smile, but beneath the sweetness it is laced with poison.

The fourth negative verbal action is *idle chatter*: speech that just fills up space without accomplishing anything. This includes gossip, meaningless chit-chat, and excessive talk about trivial topics that distract us and those around us, cluttering our minds with useless words and information.

Of the four kinds of negative speech, idle chatter is the one that we fall into most often. This is particularly true these days, with omnipresent social media feeds and celebrity culture driving us ever deeper into the realm of the superficial and the plastic. We are bombarded with idle chatter, addicted to it, and for the most part we don't seem to think there is any problem with it.

The trouble is, everyone longs for greater meaning in their lives. Your connections with other people and the intimacy you share with them – including your conversations with them – can be one of the channels through which you discover and share a sense of meaning and fulfillment. But if the speech you share is habitually devoid of meaningful content and inherently unfulfilling, then it becomes a burden upon your awareness.

The practice of mindful speech requires paying attention not only to what you talk about – which is important in itself – but also to how you speak, and why. This means being aware of the intention behind what you say. You could be talking about the deepest spiritual topic and your speech might still be idle chatter if your motivation is simply to assert your point of view or to make yourself sound smart to the other person. By the same token, you could be talking about something seemingly inane – the latest Top 40 pop song – and it might be meaningful speech if you are genuinely communicating from the heart.

Idle chatter often gets the better of us; it occupies massive sections of our mental bandwidth. It dominates our conversations with other people to such an extent that we may not even be aware that we're doing it.

Thinking back to your reflections on death and impermanence from the Second Reminder, examine your everyday speech habits and ask yourself: If I were to die right now, would I consider this conversation meaningful, or a waste of breath? If I were on my death bed looking back at my life, would I honestly feel that all the time I've spent talking about some celebrity's latest shenanigans was really time well spent?

Three Mental Actions

The last three of the ten negative actions don't necessarily involve acting with your body or your speech. They are disturbing states of mind that plant negative karmic seeds when you indulge in them.

The first negative mental action is *covetousness*. This includes the coveting thoughts you have about other people's homes, wealth, beauty, relationships, and so on. It's simply human to experience passing feelings of jealousy from time to time. But when you feed these feelings – thinking endlessly of how nice it would be if you had something that belongs to someone else – then you can spin out into obsession and lose yourself in greed and envy. You become like the beings described in the Hungry Ghost realm: tortured by hunger and thirst that can never be satisfied.

The second negative mental action is *ill will* or *malice*. This means actively wishing harm upon another person, but also includes all the malicious thoughts you have about others. You might feel irritated when prosperity comes to someone you don't like, or when someone you consider to be a bad person succeeds. Secretly, you wish their good fortune would go bust so you could watch them fall. You might even resort to plotting their downfall, scheming about ways to ensure that they suffer misfortune and failure. Or you might just stew in your own hatred and self-pity, reinforcing your personal storyline about how justified you are in disliking that person. If something bad happens to them, you take pleasure in it. That's malice, and it's toxic.

When you indulge in feelings of malice towards others, it is like swallowing poison and waiting for the other person to feel the symptoms. You are the one who is most adversely affected, because your own mind becomes a toxic swamp; you become trapped in angry story lines and mired in feelings of depression and rage. If you could see the expression of your malice reflected back to you in a mirror, you would be horrified by how it makes you look.

The third negative mental action is *wrong view*, or wallowing in delusion. This includes denying the commonsense truth of karma, saying that negative actions don't have a negative effect and positive actions don't have a positive effect. It also includes the extreme views of *eternalism* and *nihilism* described earlier, which are both equally deluded. The Buddha taught that seeing reality clearly means finding a middle path, not falling into either of these two extremes.

Practicing What You Preach

People often embark on a practice like yoga or meditation thinking that it will give them inner peace, but they remain unwilling to shine the spotlight of the practice into every corner of their lives: their actions and choices, their patterns of consumption, their sexual behavior, the way they speak to other people, the resentments and grudges they carry. Although they may study and practice diligently, they can't seem to figure out why their lives are still a mess, and why peace is so elusive. What they fail to understand is how ethical behavior steers the mind towards awakening and freedom, and how unethical behavior steers the mind towards further suffering.

To truly turn the mind in the direction of awakening and freedom, it's not enough to just refrain from negative actions. You also need to make a conscious effort to perform *virtuous* actions, which are the opposite of the ten negative actions.

On the level of physical actions, don't just refrain from killing, but protect life (including the life of our planet and its biodiversity, so much of which is in peril today). Don't just refrain from stealing, but practice generosity towards others. Don't just refrain from sexual misconduct, but be disciplined and wise with your sexual energy.

On the level of speech, don't just avoid lying, but make the effort to speak truthfully. Don't just refrain from divisive speech, but help to reconcile disputes and mend human relationships when you can. Don't just refrain from harsh speech, but actually speak in a way that puts other people's minds at ease. Don't just avoid gossip and idle chatter, but choose your topics and tone of voice to make your speech truly meaningful.

On the level of mind, don't just refrain from indulging feelings of covetousness and jealousy, but again, learn to be generous towards others – even in your thoughts. Wish others well in your thoughts, and be happy for them when they are happy. Don't just give up malice and ill-will towards others, but actually cultivate a desire to help them. And don't just give up wrong views and delusion, but do your best to develop clear seeing and authentic insight into the nature of things.

PLANTING SEEDS IN THE GARDEN OF GOOD AND EVIL

By turning the ten negative actions upside down and practicing their opposites, you do more than avoid planting negative karmic seeds; you begin proactively planting positive ones, which will certainly come to fruition at some future moment. You consciously till the garden and create the conditions – both in your outer life and in your own mindstream – for happiness and awakening to flourish.

You could meditate and do yoga and study scriptures and chant mantras until you're blue in the face, but if your everyday actions don't reflect the wisdom you seek to embody, then all your practice is just "good-for-nothing goat shit" (to borrow Patrul Rinpoche's delicate phrase once again).

Wisdom that remains theoretical and ungrounded in daily life is not really wisdom – it's just intellectual knowledge. To bring wisdom to life, you need to apply it on an everyday, kitchen-sink level, allowing it to infuse everything that you do. If you want to awaken from the trance and find true freedom, it's essential to train your mind through meditation and to cultivate the wisdom that sees reality clearly – but those things alone are not enough. You also need to ground your life on a firm ethical foundation. Ethical behavior keeps the karmic slate clean and your conscience clear, making it possible to rest your mind more easily in meditation and to see the true nature of things with greater clarity. It also makes you better prepared for that inevitable moment – in the near or distant future – when you will look death in the face and see your life flash before you. If you have charted the course of your life by your own internal ethical compass, then you will be better prepared, as Milarepa said, "to live and die without regret."

In the Lojong system of mind training taught in Tibetan Buddhism, there is a slogan: "Two activities: one at the beginning, one at the end." This slogan refers to the practice of book-ending your day to check how well your actual behavior is aligned with your intentions and aspirations. It's a simple, two-part practice. In the morning, before jumping out of bed and rushing into your day, take a moment to think about your motivation for the day. Set a heartfelt intention (or what yogis call a *Sankalpa*): "Today I will use whatever circumstances and situations arise as fuel for awakening from the trance and benefiting others as much as possible." Then, in the evening, before going to sleep, review your day and see where you succeeded and failed in honoring your intention. Give yourself credit for your positive actions, and be happy about them; and look honestly at your negative actions, resolving in your heart not to go on repeating actions that aren't in the best interest of yourself and those around you.

In old Tibet, some people would do this practice using black and white pebbles. When they reviewed their day, they would place a white pebble in the pile for each action they considered virtuous or selfless, and a black pebble for each action that was unvirtuous or self-centered. Ideally, over time, they would see the pile of pebbles getting lighter each evening, with fewer and fewer black pebbles representing negative actions. These days, instead of pebbles, you could write in a journal or make a spreadsheet on your laptop to have a digital inventory of your actions.

Ethical conduct is a prerequisite for genuine spiritual awakening. It creates the positive karmic conditions in your mind that make it possible to see reality more clearly and to free yourself from spells of self-created suffering. Unethical conduct creates a burden on your mind and heart, dragging you down to the "lower realms" of suffering and regret.

Keeping your mind aimed in the direction of truth and freedom is the whole purpose of the Four Reminders. Contemplating karma and ethical conduct makes your aim more accurate.

CONTEMPLATING THE THIRD REMINDER

Contemplation: Practicing without Confusion
Traditional teachings describe how karma plays out through rebirth and multiple lifetimes. But even if you don't believe in a literal kind of rebirth or multiple lives, consider how this principle still applies to your ordinary, everyday experience. In each moment, you are dying and being reborn in the next moment. Everything you are, down to the very cells of your body, is constantly in flux, always changing.

Your experience in any given moment is conditioned by your actions in previous moments. The cells of your body, right now, are alive as a result of past actions: the food you ate, the water you drank, the air you breathed, and even the dangers you avoided. Your mind, too, exists as it is right now because of past actions. Consider the effects on your mind of acting selfishly, motivated by greed, aggression, or addiction: how do you feel afterwards?

Now consider the effect on your mind of acting selflessly, motivated by compassion, kindness, and non-attachment: how do you feel afterwards? Which of these two feelings would you like to experience more of?

Contemplation: Karma and Habitual Patterns

Reflect on your daily life and do a mental inventory of your relationships with family, friends, coworkers, competitors, enemies, and strangers. Are there situations in which you habitually act in ways that are aggressive, impatient, clinging, addicted, or just indifferent?

What are the long-term effects of this behavior – both in terms of how it affects others, and how it affects your own state of mind? What 'realm' do you inhabit when you indulge in these kinds of actions?

Are there other situations in which you commonly express generosity, patience, and kindness? What are the effects of this behavior on you and on others? What sort of 'realm' does this create for you?

Have there been times in your life when, through your own habitual patterns, you've become stuck in a realm of suffering of your own creation? How did you get out of such a trap?

Examine your habitual patterns to see how you are accumulating positive or negative karma.

Contemplation: Seeds and Sparks

Just as a tiny seed planted in the ground can give rise to a massive tree, a small spark can start a huge fire, and a small amount of dye can color a large amount of fabric, consider how even an action that may seem insignificant at the time can dramatically color and shape your subsequent experience. Can you think of specific examples from your own life?

Contemplate the impact of small negative actions, and small positive ones. Small actions can produce very large results.

Contemplation: Examining Your Motivation

When a parent yells at a child, the net effect can be positive or negative depending on the motivation. If the parent is just impatient and angry, the effect is felt as negative; but if the child is about to step into the street without looking, or about to place their hand on a hot stove, then the parent's harsh tone of voice is actually in the child's best interest.

Can you think of examples from your own life when you acted in a way that might outwardly appear negative, but was really coming from a sincere and positive motivation?

What about the reverse – a seemingly positive action that was actually tinged with selfishness or jealousy? What role does your intention play in shaping the karmic effect that comes from an action?

Contemplation: The Ten Negative Actions

Think about each of the ten negative actions, and whether there are particular areas of your life in which you indulge in these actions.

Do you kill or steal or cheat, even on a small scale? Are all your business dealings straightforward and honest? Is your sexual conduct skillful and harmless? Do you lie to others, or indulge in character assassination or gossip about them? Do you speak harshly, in a way that hurts others' feelings? Or do you tend to slip into frequent, idle chatter just to fill up dead air space? Do you feel jealous of other people's happiness, or harbor feelings malice or ill-will towards them? Do you hold any grudges?

If you answered yes to any of the above questions, examine your conscience to see what effects these actions have on your mind. Consider how this will ripen into future experience. Contemplate the karmic results of engaging in negative actions.

Contemplation: Your Positive Karma

After contemplating the First Reminder, having developed an appreciation of your own good fortune in this life and recognizing the rare opportunity you have to wake up in this lifetime, reflect upon the amount of positive karma that was involved in getting you to this point. Are you going to squander this precious opportunity or make the best use of it? And what would making the best use of it look like? Remember, it's up to you. And everything you do matters.

Contemplate, too, the opportunities you have before you – this year, this month, this week, this day, this hour – to plant positive seeds.

As a post-meditation practice, just for today, choose one action that, for you, represents planting a positive karmic seed – and go do it. Afterwards, reflect on how it made you feel.

•••••••

For additional suggestions on contemplating the Third Reminder, refer to the accompanying Study and Discussion Guide, which you can download at:

www.thefourreminders.com

THE FOURTH REMINDER

**GOING IN CIRCLES IS POINTLESS.
WAKE UP!**

CAN'T GET NO SATISFACTION

In your entire life, have you ever really been completely satisfied with *anything* for more than a few minutes—or maybe, at best, a few hours, or a few days? Even when you experience life's finest pleasures, there is still a little nagging voice at the back of your mind, saying, "Well...this is great, but...*maybe it would be even better if only* _____" (complete the sentence). Or you start worrying about when it will end: "This is awesome, but...how long will it last? How can I guard against all the potential threats that could take this good thing away from me?"

The curse of being human is to be forever dissatisfied with what we have, to be always restlessly wishing that we had more of something, or less of something, or something better, or that we could make something last longer. This time, the Rolling Stones told the truth: as human beings it seems we just "can't get no satisfaction."

Even when things in your life are going well, there's still a subtle undercurrent of dissatisfaction: it's just not good enough yet. There's always some perceived room for improvement. You could use a little more money, or a little more time to yourself, or a little more respect and validation from others; or your relationship could be just a little better, if only the other person would change and behave as you want them to. This haunting, inescapable quality of dissatisfaction is one of the most basic forms of human suffering. The Buddha called it "all-pervasive suffering."

We live under the fairy tale-like illusion that if we could just get all the puzzle pieces lined up correctly – the right job, the right house or apartment, the right lover or husband or wife, the right car, the right pills and vitamins, the right spiritual state – then we would live happily ever after, and we wouldn't have to suffer any more. It's as if we really believe that by once and for all achieving the right combination of external conditions, we will finally create a lasting, happy, and secure existence for ourselves. Living under this illusion leaves us in a very pitiful state: perpetually yearning for a happiness that always lies just around the next corner – a dangling carrot of satisfaction that's forever just beyond reach. We spend our lives going in circles, like a dog chasing its own tail.

Many of us go down the rabbit hole and lose ourselves in the material world of appearances. We worship fast cars, designer clothes, peak experiences, mansions, money, beauty, fame, power, and sexual prowess. Our society applauds these things, giving them a totem-like status that is believed to imbue one's life with meaning, value, and purpose. To have these things is to live the dream, and to be deprived of them is a humiliation, a stigma. Many human beings are under the illusion – and make no mistake, it is an illusion, and one that is skillfully packaged and sold to us by experts – that life is really a game, like Candy Crush, and the way to live a meaningful life is to grab and devour as much candy as we can before we die.

Media and pop culture stoke the flames of this fantasy. In 21st-century society, we build hedonistic cults of celebrity around stars of reality television, movies and music. We put these stars on pedestals and worship them like gods and goddesses, telling endless stories about them

THE FOUR REMINDERS

and tracking their movements with awe and wonder. We pretend that they have perfect lives, the sort of lives we should all aspire to have. But sadly, if you scratch beneath the surface and explore their true experience, these gods and goddesses go through the same suffering as we do. They, too, experience restless dissatisfaction and longing; they feel the same desperate desire to keep what they have or to get more of it, and the same fear of losing it. From the outside, looking up at them from our lower perch on the socioeconomic ladder, their lives may look perfect; but on the inside, they are just as lost and confused as the rest of us. Sometimes even more so. "More money, more problems," as a famous song reminds us.

What I'm about to say may feel like a big disappointment, but here's the sad truth of it. As a human being, you will probably never get all your puzzle pieces lined up correctly. As soon as you put one piece in place, another piece falls out somewhere else, and you have to scramble to replace it. Even if you were to win the lottery and suddenly fall into the perfect life – able to buy your way into all the good experiences and buy your way out of the bad ones – there would still be one problem: it doesn't last. You still have to accept the sufferings of change, impermanence, sickness, old age, and death. Whatever you hold dear will eventually decay and slip away from your grasp, and death brings an end to even the most charmed life.

Not even our celebrity gods and goddesses can escape that. They may try to hold on to their youthful beauty – which is so often the source of their allure and power – but no matter how many facelifts or injections or implant surgeries they undergo to prop up the facade just a little bit longer, they cannot postpone the inevitable. Gravity always wins.

Humans don't like change. Change is uncertain and unfamiliar, and that feels threatening. This is why you craft so many strategies for resisting and denying change. You try to solidify things in a way that makes you feel happy and secure – and keep them that way. Fixated on external things and always leaning into the future, towards some idealized state of bliss that is promised in some future moment, you forget that the key to contentment is already in your hands. You wander far from home in search of something else, something better, but no matter how far you roam you never arrive anywhere else but in the present moment. In the words of an old country song, you're always "looking for love in all the wrong places" – never realizing that it starts right here, in your own heart and mind.

Fear and Attachment
The great 11th-century Buddhist meditation master Tilopa said to his student, Naropa: "You are not bound by appearances; you are bound by clinging. Cut through your clinging, Naropa."

What Tilopa meant by "appearances" are all the pleasant and unpleasant experiences that come and go in life; all the things that arise in our experience of the phenomenal world. Like Naropa, you are not really bound by things or experiences, which come and go. You are bound, and you suffer, because you don't really want to admit that things and experiences change, that they come and go, and you form attachment and aversion to them. When nice things or pleasant experiences come along, you get stuck in attachment to them and craving more of them, and attachment and craving to things that change makes you suffer. And when unpleasant or painful things come along, such as being sick or being stuck in situations you don't like, you feel strong aversion towards your experience, piling emotional suffering on top of the actual pain itself.

Because things come and go and you can never seem to find solid ground beneath your feet, you experience fear. Like most people, the list of things you fear is probably a fairly long one: death, illness, pain, financial insecurity,

THE FOUR REMINDERS

ridicule and embarrassment, loneliness, abandonment, heartbreak...surely your list could go on.

But here's a secret: you can only fear losing something to which you are attached. The magic prescription for reducing fear and suffering is really quite simple, and goes back to what Tilopa said to Naropa: stop focusing on appearances, and cut through your attachments to them.

If life has smiled on you by bringing you a beautiful car, a great job, a wonderful spouse, or a sexy body – great! Enjoy it while it lasts. You won't necessarily suffer because you are gifted with these material comforts. You will only suffer from them if you cling to them, hold them tightly, take refuge in them and convince yourself that they are a reliable source of meaning and a lasting source of security and contentment. The truth is that they are none of those things. Material pleasures are fun while they last, but when you cling to them and look for your life's purpose in hoarding more and more of them, you create your own future suffering.

We all long for homes and wealth and the pleasures of tasty food; we want to be liked and respected; we yearn to be beautiful and powerful and to get what we want. This is human nature. In fact, it's animal nature; even primates swinging from trees demonstrate the desire for power, comfort, and social status. These are instinctual drives that are perhaps more deeply embedded in our biology than we realize.

But if you inquire a bit more deeply, you discover that these things, as pleasant as they may be, are not reliable refuges from life's unpleasant truths. They may provide fleeting moments of happiness that lull you into a false sense of security, but the unpleasant truths you're trying to distract yourself from are still there. No matter how much good stuff you get, you always want more; the good stuff you get doesn't last as long as you want it to; and you are always fearful of losing whatever good stuff you have. And bad stuff has a way of creeping in, sooner or later, to spoil the party.

The Fourth Reminder doesn't ask you to give up your material possessions, put on a monk's robes, and live in a monastery like I did. It doesn't ask you to wear a hair shirt and flagellate yourself to mortify the flesh like a medieval Christian mendicant. But it does ask you to take an honest, hard look at your own attachments, and begin to loosen their grip upon your psyche. If you're ever going to stop going in circles, you need to figure out if you're chasing your own tail, and why.

The Buddha taught that you should tread a middle path in life: a balanced way of being in the world that avoids the extreme of ascetic renunciation on the one hand, and the extreme of materialistic indulgence and hedonism on the other. Acknowledging the truth of impermanence and the reality of suffering, you can remain open to the experience of whatever passing pleasures and disappointments life brings your way. Let them come and let them go.

Becoming an "Insider"

The human search for contentment is the natural expression of our life force. All living creatures want to be basically happy and at peace. The problem is that our search for contentment is habitually misdirected outside, when it should be directed inside. One of the Tibetan words for a spiritual seeker is *ngakpa*, which literally means "insider" – someone who goes within.

You could spend your whole life going in circles, chasing external fulfillment, like a dog chasing its tail. Or you could stop, turn your attention inside, and discover the true source of contentment. The Fourth Reminder is really about turning away from trivial pursuits, and towards the one truly important thing: waking up and being free.

Being an "insider" doesn't mean that you don't need to focus on properly maintaining your outer circumstances and obligations, or that you should be withdrawn from engagement with the world. Quite the opposite: when you contemplate karma and realize how interdependent we all are, you begin to see ever more clearly how many things need your attention – from meeting your own basic material needs and supporting your loved ones, to addressing social and economic injustice, environmental degradation, political corruption, and more.

The Buddha described the ideal of the Bodhisattva, someone who strives for awakening and freedom not in order to leave behind this world full of suffering beings, but in order to turn around and relieve the suffering of other beings even more effectively from the perspective of being awakened and seeing clearly what needs to be done.

Being an 'insider' isn't going to magically solve every problem. To a person of color dealing with our society's systemic racism, turning within is not going to erase the cruelty they face when they simply walk down the street or apply for a job. To someone stricken with real depression, it would be glib and insulting to say, "Oh, just look for contentment inside, and snap out of it!" Turning within is not going to bring back any of the vanishing species of animals that are going extinct on our planet at an alarming rate. To address these and many other real-world problems, we need to remain engaged with our world – now more than ever before.

What being an "insider" does do is give you a radically different perspective on your own experience. It makes you better appreciate the value of your own life, and stop taking it for granted. It reveals the truth of impermanence, driving you to live with a greater sense of urgency. It makes you reflect on ethics and karma, so you align your behavior with your values. And it refocuses your priorities, so you stop going in pointless circles and start pursuing what's truly meaningful. No matter who you are or what your circumstances, the Four Reminders are as true for you as they are for anyone else alive on earth.

THE GREAT WAY IS NOT DIFFICULT FOR THOSE WITH NO PREFERENCES

When I lived in the monastery, one of the most profound and challenging aspects of our training as monks and nuns was the practice of "choicelessness."

As humans, we ordinarily spend a vast amount of time and energy – perhaps even the majority of it – making choices and fussing over our personal preferences about everything from our food to our clothing to the creature comforts of our home. Much of our energy goes into trying to get our way and impose our personal preferences on other people, and negotiating all the conflicts that arise from clashing preferences. Your partner feels like eating sushi tonight and watching a certain TV show, but you feel like eating pasta and watching a different TV show. Boom! Conflict.

Like Goldilocks in the children's fable, you jump constantly from one experience to another, always searching for the experience that's "just right" – the one that perfectly matches your personal preferences. You spend your life trying to make yourself comfortable by selecting and acquiring the objects that meet your criteria. But your

THE FOUR REMINDERS

preferences are fickle and quixotic, and things often don't live up to your expectations. The movie you so looked forward to – and coerced your friends into seeing with you – turns out to be dreadful, and you leave the theater feeling disappointed (and chastened by your friends for selecting such a bad film). The pasta that pleased you yesterday gives you indigestion today. The shirt you loved so much when you bought it last season looks dreadful when you put it on now – clearly a mistaken fashion choice.

At the monastery we were forced to drop these self-defeating habits altogether and to work, instead, with the discipline of choicelessness. In a monastery, this discipline is applied, somewhat ruthlessly, to every aspect of your life as a monk or nun:

- **Appearance**: Forget about how you would prefer to look. Leave your fancy hair products behind. Shave your head like everyone else. Forget about jewelry and make-up and accessories and your favorite clothing, and T-shirts with cute or funny messages on them – they're not allowed. Wear the simple robes that are given to you, which look exactly like everyone else's robes. Stop trying to be unique and to 'express yourself' with your appearance. That's just your ego playing games to impress other people and make you feel better about yourself.

- **Food**: Forget about your food preferences. Eat only the food that is prepared for you, and eat it only when it's placed in front of you at the appointed hour. If you don't like the food, you are cordially invited to keep your complaints to yourself. Or don't eat. Go read a book instead. Or meditate.

- **Sleep**: Forget about your creature comforts. Sleep in the bed that is offered to you, and be thankful you have one. If you don't like your roommate's snoring, you are cordially invited to get over it. Try wearing earplugs.

- **Schedule**: Forget about sleeping in, or planning your day according to your mood. Wake up with the others and follow the schedule everyone else follows. Go to morning chants. Do your chores. Do your work. Do your meditation practice. Go to sleep. Wake up and do it again. Don't like the schedule? You are cordially invited to get used to it.

- **Entertainment**: Forget about escaping into the movie of your choice whenever you feel like you need a break from it all. You can watch the single film that's provided once a week on Friday evening – which is selected by majority vote – or you can leave the room. Try going to bed early.

Life Does Not Revolve Around You

You learn very quickly in the monastery that life does not revolve around you and your personal preferences. As in the military, life in a monastery is rigorously structured and there's a program to be followed for pretty much everything. That's necessary for the functioning of the monastery; but until you understand that and accept it, your ego resists. Eventually you learn one of two things: either how to get with the program and be generally okay with it, or how to continue making yourself miserable by struggling against it. Those are your options. Which one is more appealing? (Of course, there's also a third option – to give up your robes and leave the monastery – which, honestly, a few people did once they realized what they had gotten themselves into. The disciplined life of a monk or nun is certainly not for everyone.)

That may sound harsh, and in some ways it is. But when you actually embrace choicelessness as a discipline, a

THE FOUR REMINDERS

form of spiritual training, it can open you up in unexpected ways. You start to see that the quick thrill of getting what you wanted pales next to the deeper, abiding sense of contentment and peace that comes from being okay with what is, without all of your habitual complaints and resistance.

You've spent your whole life trying to get everything and everyone around you to align with your personal preferences. How's that working out for you?

Maybe it's time to consider the possibility that this enslavement to your preferences – this endless cycle of picking and choosing, accepting and rejecting – has caused more trouble than it is worth. What would happen if you were to drop all that and simply let things be as they are?

In the monastery this meant that yes, in fact, you may still dislike the burritos that are served every two weeks, like clockwork. You may still dislike the film that was chosen by the group for movie night. You may dislike the schedule, and feel a burning resentment at being forced out of your warm bed and into the cold meditation hall for 6:00 a.m. practice every day. But after a while you start to see that your personal preferences are just that: they're *your* personal preferences. You begin to understand how you are ruled by your preferences; how they make you miserable because you take them so seriously and believe that life should be served to you, at all times, your way.

But when you stop complaining about the violation of your personal preferences – that is, you stop whining and get with the program – then you stop making yourself and those around you miserable. There is a certain kind of freedom that can only be discovered when you stop being so tied up in your own ego's habits and instincts.

And so you discover that a burrito is not the dramatic culinary insult that you were making it out to be. It's just food, after all. You could choose to eat the burrito anyway, without throwing a temper tantrum. You might even experience a faint glimmer of gratitude that, unlike so many other people in the world who suffer from hunger, you have a burrito to eat in the first place. What's that, you say? A burrito is not what you wanted? *So what?* Are you really still operating under the illusion that life is supposed to give you everything you want, all the time? Grow up.

Choicelessness in Everyday Life

You don't have to go to the extremes of shaving your head and living in a monastery to work with the discipline of choicelessness. You can experiment with it in your everyday life. Each day, take one small opportunity to notice when your ego is trying to manipulate a situation to go your way – and when you notice that, see if you can drop it.

If there's a discussion between you and your partner or your friends about what movie to see on a Friday night, or what to eat for dinner, experiment with making a conscious decision to drop your personal agenda and just do whatever they want to do. Observe your ego kicking and screaming like a brat as you eat the burrito. Eat it anyway. It's just food. What's the big deal? Notice, afterwards, how your whole world did not, in fact, come crashing down. Sometimes a burrito is just a burrito.

The spiritual path is about learning to recognize and peel away the layers of your individual ego – with all its demands and distortions, its likes and dislikes – in order to uncover the egoless, undifferentiated Being that is your true nature. As long as you are caught up in the lifelong momentum of trying to satisfy ego's preferences and keep ego happy, it will be hard to make much progress at peeling away those layers. Surrendering to choicelessness, moment by moment, is a discipline that can help you peel away the layers of the onion, one by one.

It's a lifelong practice, because the onion of the ego seems to have unlimited layers. But the more you can drop the perpetual struggle to acquire what you like and push

THE FOUR REMINDERS

away what you dislike, the easier it becomes to glimpse the truth and to discover a deeper, more abiding form of contentment that doesn't depend so heavily on external conditions.

Seng-ts'an, one of the ancient forefathers of Zen, put it like this (beautifully translated from Chinese by the late Richard B. Clarke):

"The Great Way is not difficult for those who have no preferences. When love and hate are both absent, everything becomes clear and undisguised. Make the smallest distinction, however, and heaven and earth are set infinitely apart. If you wish to see the truth, then hold no opinion for or against. The struggle of what one likes and what one dislikes is the disease of the mind."

Stop Making a Big Deal

All living beings are hardwired to seek pleasure and comfort and to avoid discomfort and pain. But we humans have developed a greater variety of ways to carry out this prime directive. We are exceptionally good at it, and extremely habituated.

If you practice mindfulness meditation, this is something you can witness happening in real time during your meditation sessions. You experience the slightest discomfort arising in the body, and your immediate impulse is to fidget and shift in your seat to make it go away. You're visited by unpleasant emotional states, or thoughts that you label as bad or unwanted, and you try to bludgeon your mind into submission through fierce concentration. When you are lucky enough to experience a very pleasant, peaceful feeling in meditation, you immediately glom onto it and try to sustain it.

If you practice enough, though, you begin to witness something else: the constant, moment-to-moment, instant-to-instant arising and passing away of thoughts, feelings and sensations. Like the weather, experiences in the mind come and go – sometimes they're bright and sunny, and other times they're dark and stormy. You can try to prepare for the weather, and adapt to it once it arrives, but you can't really control it. You can complain about the weather, or sing its praises. Either way, the weather doesn't change for you. It changes all by itself, in its own time. After enough witnessing of thoughts and feelings arising and passing in the mind, you simply stop investing them with so much unnecessary importance.

Our normal pattern – so deeply ingrained that most of the time we do it on autopilot, without even noticing we are doing it – is to make a big deal out of our experience. Good or bad, happy or sad, pleasant or painful, in our minds we exaggerate both the significance and the duration of whatever experience is happening at the moment. And we react – or over-react – accordingly. An itch arises, and we scratch it reflexively, without thinking about it. But a shift takes place when we start to simply notice what is happening in our experience, without reacting.

Mindfulness training awakens in us this newfound capacity to stop making a big deal out of every thought or feeling that arises. The itch still comes, but you pause long enough to simply pay attention to the sensation without reacting immediately. Maybe you scratch it, maybe you don't. But you recognize that you are not, in fact, going to die of discomfort if you don't scratch it. Your back hurts, and you either move or don't move to alleviate the pain – but if you move, you do it consciously, with awareness. A feeling of sadness or joy comes over you, and you realize you can simply be there with the feeling – nothing in particular has to be done with it. An online troll says something trollish, and instead of reacting in a flash of anger you pause long enough to ask yourself whether engaging with an online troll is a valuable use of your time.

You start to see that your own thoughts and feelings, like everything else, are momentary. They change all the time. You don't have to make a bigger deal out of them than they really are.

Practicing this way during meditation is only a form of training. The purpose of the training is to be able to apply it in everyday life, when situations arise that either give you great pleasure or cause pain or stress. With practice, you can catch yourself in the very act of glomming onto your experience and starting to make a big deal out of it. You can observe the patterns of attachment and aversion that arise within your mind, and you can decide how much energy you really want to invest in them. And, in that gap, you can choose to react in ways that serve the greater good, rather than flying on autopilot.

SIX REALMS OF THE MIND

Western science takes a largely materialistic approach to explaining our mental and emotional states, relating them primarily to the body and to neurochemical processes. Modern neuroscience sees little or no difference between the "mind" and the physical brain and nervous system.

The psychology taught by the Buddha, on the other hand, says that while mind and body are enmeshed in a mutually dependent relationship, they are not necessarily one and the same. "Not same, not different" might be the maddening, Sphinx-like answer given by the Buddha to the eternal riddle of the mind-body relationship. There is, at any rate, a significant feedback loop between the two: your mental and physical habits reinforce each other. This feedback loop can be a virtuous circle or a vicious one, depending on what habits you cultivate.

Through years and years of habituation – training yourself in certain patterns of thought and emotion – you develop a 'set-point,' a more or less hardened, habitual way of relating to your experience. Your set-point, whether it's high or low or somewhere in-between, can appear (to you and to those around you) to be a very solid, very real thing. You may be very good at justifying it, explaining why you

THE FOUR REMINDERS

cannot deviate very much from it. Often this justification takes the form of stories you tell yourself and others about how the world has done you wrong.

Your wounds and your pride are central to your sense of identity; they are the core around which you weave the cocoon of your own suffering. Eckhart Tolle calls this the "pain-body," an invisible but pervasive cloud of mental anguish and sorrow that you carry with you everywhere you go – like the unbathed character Pig-Pen in the *Peanuts* cartoons, who is trailed at all times by a cloud of his own dirt and stink. You project the shadow of your pain-body onto the situations and people you encounter, unintentionally sowing discord and chaos in your relationships. And it all comes back, again, to the Third Reminder: karma.

A person who repeatedly indulges in anger and aggression becomes more and more easily angered and provoked to aggression – until he finds himself locked in a hell-realm state of mind where everything constantly enrages him and he's at war with everyone in his life. A person who repeatedly indulges in anxiety, rumination, and despair becomes more and more easily trapped in those feelings – until she finds herself mired in the quicksand of an ongoing depression that seems, to her, inescapable.

What began as a small seed of karma becomes a pattern, and finally it solidifies into a whole way of being in the world – a psychological 'realm' defined by a particular quality of experience. Whichever direction you roll the snowball of karma, it grows and grows, until what started as a small snowball in your hands eventually becomes a giant boulder that overshadows you and becomes the only thing you can see. Once you've entered fully into one of the mind's realms, it becomes difficult to find the exit door.

Your set-point helps to define the psychological realm in which you live – a hell realm, a god realm, or something in-between. From that familiar starting place, you use

SIX REALMS OF THE MIND

everything that happens to you as bricks in the walls of identity that you are constantly building around yourself. The thicker and higher you build the walls, the harder it becomes to see beyond them. In fact, you forget that you are even building them. In a kind of self-fulfilling prophecy, you become totally convinced that the identity you've built is who you really are. But your belief in the solidity of the walls of your realm is the only thing that keeps you trapped there. You are your own jailer. From the inside, the walls that enclose you appear to be "out there," and so you search "out there" for freedom. But you are the only one who could possibly hold the key to such a self-made prison.

The Buddha's profound teachings on the nature of mind tell us that the perception of separateness that you habitually experience between yourself and the world outside is mistaken. At a deeper level of your being, there is no clear separation, no solid self that can be pinpointed and isolated from the web of interdependent causes and conditions giving rise to your experience in each moment. Your inner world and your outer world are in a constant state of feedback and interplay, and the 'internal' karma of your thoughts, emotions, and habitual patterns is mirrored back to you through the 'external' karma of your experiences. You imagine that there is a sharp dividing line between your inner state of mind and your outer experience – a clear separation between the mind and its encompassing world – but when you look closely, you can't find exactly where the line is drawn. The realm you create inside your own mind is mirrored back to you in your life through the habitual way you experience and react to your world.

According to Tibetan Buddhist philosophy, this self-imprisonment comes in six basic styles or flavors, which are the six realms described earlier in this book, in the chapter on the First Reminder. Sentient beings continually go in circles, cycling through these six realms – getting stuck for a while in this one, then moving on to get stuck in another one.

The six realms describe the spectrum of possible experiences you could have as a sentient being. Each realm reflects a particular emotional quality that you experience right here in our familiar, human world. Based on your mental and volitional habits, you solidify yourself into states of mind that color your perception of the world. Sometimes this habit energy can be so dense that you might spend your whole life stuck in one particular realm, seeing everything through the thick filter of karma you've created for yourself.

The Hell Realm

The lowest of the six realms is the hell realm, described in Tibetan Buddhist texts as a place of constant torment and intense suffering without relief. The dominant emotional theme of the hell realm is anger and hatred.

Of all the six realms, the iconography and descriptions of the hell realms are the most vivid and graphic – full of evangelical hellfire and brimstone and the frightening tortures inflicted on hell-beings. Ancient texts speak of eighteen different hell realms – eight cold hells, eight hot hells, and two bordering hells – with scary names like the Crushing Hell, the Howling Hell, the Hell of Ultimate Torment, the Hell of Burst Blisters, the Hell of Chattering Teeth, and so on. Depictions of these realms are straight out of a blood-and-guts Hollywood horror movie.

In one hell realm you repeatedly drown in rivers of putrid, rotting corpses, while in another, you are cut into pieces, then put back together, and cut to pieces again, over and over. In one hell realm you must crawl across beds of razors, and in still another you are repeatedly crushed between stone mountains that slam together.

Looking beyond the gory specificity of these portrayals, it's not impossible to relate to the experiences they depict.

SIX REALMS OF THE MIND

If you simply look around, right here in our human realm on planet Earth, you can find many places where people are locked in seemingly endless struggle and misery. Untold numbers of people on our planet are afflicted by starvation, epidemics of disease, perpetual warfare and genocide, and unthinkable natural or man-made disasters.

You don't have to imagine a hell realm as a supernatural, mysterious dimension of existence completely separate from our own human realm. Hell could be – and frequently is – right here on Earth, in our own minds. A story from the Zen tradition illustrates this.

A great Samurai warrior went to visit a Zen master and asked the master to teach him about heaven and hell. The Zen master looked up from his tea, casting the warrior a withering glance, and replied condescendingly, "I couldn't possibly teach you anything about heaven and hell. You're far too stupid to comprehend my teachings."

The warrior's face turned red with rage and humiliation, and he drew his sword to cut off the head of the Zen master. But then the master raised his index finger and pointed at the warrior in his rage, poised to commit murder.

"That," he said, "is hell."

This direct and experiential teaching instantly cut through the warrior's rage, and he understood that he had created his own hell realm through his emotional reaction. He laid his sword on the ground and knelt before the Zen master, joining his palms together in a gesture of gratitude and humility. The Zen master pointed his index finger at the warrior again, and said:

"That is heaven."

Like the Samurai warrior, you unwittingly create your own realms, both heavenly and hellish, through your emotional reactivity and the actions that follow.

The Hungry Ghost Realm

Just above the hell realm is the hungry ghost realm, characterized by overwhelming desire, craving, attachment and poverty mentality. Ancient texts portray hungry ghosts as suffering extreme anguish because they are terribly hungry and thirsty, but their mouths are so small and their throats so thin that they cannot swallow much of anything. For a hungry ghost, there is never enough – no satisfaction, and no rest.

This is a good description of what happens to us when we get trapped in poverty mentality and depression. It's Tara Brach's "trance of unworthiness" – the pervasive feeling that there's something fundamentally wrong with you, that you're not sufficient to face the circumstances of your life. Like a hungry ghost, when you get trapped in poverty mentality, you cannot allow positive thoughts or emotions into your bubble because you are so focused on what's wrong with you, or what's wrong with life.

If you have ever held a conversation with someone who was trapped in a deep, chronic depression, or with an addict who was in the throes of an active addiction, then you know very well what a hungry ghost looks like. If you've ever been one of those people yourself, then you also know what being a hungry ghost feels like.

The Animal Realm

The hallmark of the animal realm, in the Tibetan Buddhist view, is ignorance. An animal's prime directive is survival: eat, avoiding being eaten, sleep, reproduce, and find ways to stay warm in the winter and cool in the summer.

You're living in the animal realm when you devote all your attention to the pursuit of "creature comforts," or when you are unable to see past your mundane concerns, as if your nose is to the ground. This happens when you get too caught up in your routines – running on the hamster wheel of work and activities – and you don't even notice the passage of time.

Suddenly, in a moment of clarity, you realize that months or years or decades have gone by. As in the Talking Heads song, you look around in confusion and ask yourself, "Well, how did I get here?"

You've been living in the animal realm, just surviving and meeting basic needs. Then you wake up one day and wonder: "OMG. WTF am I doing with my life?"

The Human Realm

The dominant theme in the human realm is desire, as well as dissatisfaction, because our desires can never be fulfilled in a truly complete or lasting way.

On the positive side, the human realm is said to be the realm with the greatest potential for awakening and liberation, because right here in the Goldilocks zone – smack in the middle of the six realms – you have just the right balance of happiness and suffering. Unlike beings in the three lower realms, you have some breathing room and leisure; it's not all suffering. You have opportunities to work towards awakening and freedom. And unlike the beings in the god realms, you have just enough suffering to be *motivated* to work towards that freedom. If you had no suffering whatsoever, you would be like the gods – smug and self-satisfied and lazy, with no motivation to grow or change.

Again, it's not difficult to see how this works in our experience. If you tell someone who is suffering from extreme hunger or illness, or someone who has been victimized by abuse or warfare, that they should just forget about all that and strive for awakening, it would strike them as condescending, naïve or even insulting. The circumstances of their suffering consume their attention so fully that they have no leisure to entertain such ideas. On the other hand, try telling someone who is living the high life at the moment, and is flourishing and successful, that they should just forget about all that and strive for awakening. Why bother trying to wake up when the dream is so pleasant?

It's only when we are in the middle, in the human realm – when we have the right balance of suffering and leisure – that we have both the motivation and the capacity to work towards our freedom.

The Jealous God Realm

Between the human realm and the god realm, in traditional depictions of the six realms, is the jealous god (or demigod) realm, where the dominant emotional theme is jealousy. Things in the demigod realm are not quite as nice and shiny and fresh as they are in the god realm, and so the beings there feel restless and jealous of the gods above them, who seem to have it all. They constantly pick fights and go to war with the gods in order to try to take back what they believe is rightfully theirs.

A traditional image used to depict this struggle is a tree whose roots are in the demigod realm, but whose branches and leaves and fruits are in the god realm. The beings below in the demigod realm see the gods above enjoying the fruits of their labor, while they have nothing, and they are enraged.

Again, you don't need to look far to see how this dynamic plays out right here in our human realm. Consider the Middle East, which has been the source of much of the industrialized world's petroleum resources. Oil from the Middle East has been one of the taproots of Western industry and affluence since the mid-twentieth century. Yet, with some notable exceptions, the majority of people in the Middle East do not enjoy the affluence of Western lifestyles. Poverty and conflict over resources and land is wide-spread; warfare has reduced entire countries to rubble and sent millions of refugees fleeing for their lives. It's not hard to imagine that some people living in that region would feel resentment towards people in Western countries for this imbalanced situation.

You get trapped in the jealous god realm when you develop chronic anger and frustration over unfair situations and perceived insults. This happens often in the workplace, when companies have many layers of management. As an employee you look up at the layers of management above you and you feel resentful. You work longer hours than they do, but you get paid less. Income inequality is a real injustice, it's not imaginary. But letting your anger about the inequality overtake your mind is what brings you into the jealous god realm.

The God Realm

In Buddhist cosmology, the gods live extremely long and pleasurable lives, blissed out and free from troubles or cares. They have perfect health, comfort, wealth, fame, and happiness all the time. The dominant emotional theme in the god realm is pride. Sounds nice, doesn't it? Sort of like everyone's idea of Plan A for living a good life. There are just two problems with Plan A.

First, because the gods are so blissed out in their pleasures and comforts and diversions, they have little motivation or inclination to pursue any sort of spiritual awakening. They are a bit too smug and satisfied with their own circumstances to want to change anything. They're having a really sweet dream, and waking up from it would be a bummer.

Second, even the god realm is not immune to the law of impermanence. The gods are said to have extremely long lives by human standards, but they are not immortal. The day inevitably comes when the karma that landed them in the god realm runs out, and they must face death like any other being. And from the top of the wheel, there is nowhere for them to go but down.

As with all the other realms, you can experience a god-realm state of mind right here in your human life. You might enjoy a temporary god-like experience if you manage to acquire great money, fame and power. The illusion of security provided by these material comforts allows you to live in a bubble where you remain largely unfazed by the daily struggles that ordinary people face. In fact, this sort of god-like existence is held up in our culture as the ideal of "the good life," something we all should strive to attain. Sometimes our whole life's energy is spent trying to build this insulated cocoon of pleasure and safety.

Six Realms, Six States of Mind

The old texts from Tibet depicted these six realms as literal places, dimensions of existence inhabited by classes of beings who all share similar karma. Putting a more contemporary, psychological spin on the six realms, we can view them as six states of mind that we experience right here in our human existence. Either way, the message is the same. The six realms are different manifestations or flavors of the game of ego: ways of fixating and solidifying our minds into habitual patterns that define our experience. Some of these states may be abhorrent to us while others are attractive, but they are all just part of the trance that keeps us spinning on the hamster wheel of suffering, going in pointless circles. They are traps that we set for ourselves and then stumble into and become caught, having forgotten that we set the traps in the first place.

FREEDOM IS AN INSIDE JOB

Ordinarily when we talk about freedom we mean something that comes from outside. It's given to us, or we fight for it, or we earn it somehow. We often think of freedom as the right to do whatever we want (within the reasonable limits imposed by law and society).

But the kind of freedom we talk about on the spiritual path doesn't come from outside. It isn't given to us by anyone else, and it doesn't even really depend all that much on external circumstances.

It's a job for an "insider," a *ngakpa*. True freedom is less about being free to do what we want and more about setting ourselves free from all the forms of internal conditioning that keep us imprisoned in the six realms of psychological and emotional suffering. It's the freedom of letting go of the familiar and stepping into Mystery.

What happens when you drop down beneath your habitual drive for security, safety, and comfort? You touch in with the vast, open Mystery that was always there, and in that Mystery there is a freedom that surpasses understanding. Imagine what this very moment would feel like if you could suddenly throw off your protective shell and taste ultimate freedom – right here, right now.

THE FOUR REMINDERS

Imagine being free from the mind's obsessive thinking. What if you could drop into a natural stillness and silence in which the mind is aware and relaxed, without chatter, without commentary?

What about freedom from troubling emotions, like greed, anger, jealousy, and hatred? How would you feel if the waters of your mind were not whipped into their usual frenzy of agitated thoughts and emotions?

Freedom from judgment – that's a big one. Look at how you constantly judge and evaluate yourself and others. What if, for just one moment, you could drop your compulsive need to be the judge of everything?

Can you even imagine being free from caring what other people think about you? How much time do you spend trapped in worrying about other people's evaluations of you, and trying to manipulate their perceptions to make a good impression? Wouldn't it be sort of glorious to experience, if only for a moment, the freedom of being unconcerned with everyone else's opinions of you?

And your own opinions – how heavy are they? You have opinions about everything under the sun, and you take your opinions so seriously, as if each one were the gospel truth. But if you can relate openly to the Mystery underlying your experience, you start to see that your opinions and judgments are like a cloud of biting insects, an irritating drain on your attention and a veil that obscures reality.

Imagine the freedom of just being here, in the present moment, without worry or anxiety about the future and without regret or resentment about the past. How much time do you spend imprisoned in mental scenarios of past and future that take you out of a lived awareness of what's actually happening in the present moment?

Imagine being free of your bad habits – and your good habits, for that matter – freedom from all forms of habit energy. Imagine being spontaneously, freshly present for your experience without the enslavement of your own conditioning.

Imagine freedom from the need to be a certain kind of person – a good person, a spiritual person, an enlightened person. What if you could be free, just for this moment, from all the trips you lay on yourself about who you think you are supposed to be?

What about freedom from the need to be in control, or from the idea that you were ever in control in the first place, or that control is really even possible? Does it threaten your ego to think of not being in control? Count the ways in which you are trying to manipulate and control your experience in this very moment.

Imagine freedom from the need to be right, and to know all the answers. That's the kicker. Right here, standing at the edge of the Mystery that's unfolding in your experience at this moment and at every moment, can you swallow your pride and admit to yourself how little you actually know about anything? And can you experience *not-knowing* as the freedom it actually is? As Kris Kristofferson and Janis Joplin sang, "Freedom's just another word for nothing left to lose."

The tragicomedy of being human is that most of the things we ordinarily think will make us free only ensnare us more deeply in prisons of our own making. True freedom is when we peel away all the layers of conditioning so that we have nothing left to lose, and we rest in the great Mystery – the open, empty, silent space of our heart and mind.

That's true freedom. But to the ego, it looks like surrender.

WHAT BRINGS YOU HERE?

Idle curiosity is generally not what brings us to the path of awakening. Most of us step onto the spiritual path after something – or a series of somethings – has driven us to it. Life's pressures and irritations have become too much; or something cherished – a job, a relationship, a state of physical health – has fallen apart, or seems in danger of falling apart. We come seeking answers, and relief.

You might be driven to the path by a slight but chronic sense of discomfort and restlessness that always seems to be there in the background of your life, or you might be driven by an intense and urgent sense of panic in reaction to current events. Either way, you come to the path looking for a better way to live, a way to ease your suffering. A sense of desperation drives you to finally seek out wisdom and awakening.

Desperation gets a bad rap in our society. We are supposed to be cool, calm, collected, and in control – and someone who is desperate has lost all those qualities. *He is pathetic, his life is out of control, he's a mess, he's losing it, he's desperate. Keep away from him, it might be contagious.*

But a little desperation is not a sign of failure; it is actually a gift. From desperation the genuine motivation can arise to change and relinquish old habitual patterns that no longer serve your growth. After passing through the dark night of the soul you can more deeply experience the miracle of the dawn.

Besides, if things are just peachy-keen and there's no sense of urgency at all to your spiritual search, then why bother with all this study and contemplation and meditation? It would be easier and more fun to just go shopping, or turn on the TV. Plug into the Matrix and go back to sleep.

Without feeling a little desperation, you have no sense of urgency, no compelling desire to grow or change, no commitment to step beyond your habitual patterns. You are lukewarm, and your spiritual path is half-hearted. You might dabble in studying or practicing spiritual teachings out of intellectual curiosity, without any real idea why you're doing it. But desperation brings things into sharp focus.

When someone is addicted to drugs, he lives in denial of his problem until things get bad enough that reality starts to pierce through the bubble of delusion. At some point, slowly or suddenly, it becomes impossible for him to go on living in denial. But usually he has to become a little bit desperate before he gets there. He has to hit bottom in order to be jarred into seeking a way back up, a way out of his self-made prison. His sense of desperation gives rise to a genuine and strong motivation to change, and that is the moment when recovery becomes possible: when he admits his problem and asks for help. But until he feels that strong motivation to change coming from within, he can talk all he wants about recovery – but he will just be blowing hot air.

On the spiritual path, there are a lot of people blowing hot air – just as in other realms of human endeavor. There are a lot of people acting cool, calm, collected, in the know, and in control. But beware of people who pretend to have everything under control. Someone who shows a

THE FOUR REMINDERS

little bit of desperation, someone who has struggled and who doubts himself sometimes – someone who bears a few scars from his journey through the dark night of the soul – may be a more reliable friend in spiritual matters.

The Buddha was desperate. Why else would he have done what he did? The Buddha left behind his life as a prince and his comfortable, luxurious palace life. He gave up sex and romance and money and power and fame, and set out as a penniless beggar on a lonely, difficult and uncompromising quest for spiritual realization. Why?

Only out of desperation would a person take such a radical, nearly unthinkable leap into the unknown. Suffering punctured the illusory bubble of luxury and comfort in which he lived, and it pierced his heart. Desperate to find the truth and to follow the path of awakening and freedom from suffering, he chose to walk away from his pampered, sheltered life.

If you reflect back to the time when you first set out on the spiritual path, you can probably connect that impulse to some kind of suffering you were experiencing in your life, some subtle or acute sense of desperation that led you to seek out something that might help you. But after you've been on the spiritual path for a while, it's easy to forget your original motivation. When things are going well, you no longer feel quite as desperate as you did before. Your outward circumstances might improve, your mind might become a little calmer, and you may be more at peace with yourself – and these are all great things. But along the way, you start to lose touch with the strong motivation to change that you felt when you set out on this path. As you move further and further away from that original spark of desperation, it becomes easy to drift into complacency.

If you feel a little bit of desperation on your spiritual path, a sense of urgency about it, count your lucky stars. That's basically what the Four Reminders are trying to get you to feel. Let that feeling be the fuel that lights your motivation to change and grow, and take whatever steps are needed in order to make that change and growth happen. Let desperation be the force that propels you forward into action and into awakening.

And if you've been on the path for a while and you've forgotten what it was like to feel desperate, try to get that old feeling back. If you've slipped into complacency about your spiritual growth, remember why you started on this journey in the first place.

YOU MIGHT AS WELL BURST OUT LAUGHING

The Four Reminders call on you to jettison from your life everything that acts as a distraction or hindrance to the goal of awakening, and to apply yourself with effort to your spiritual practice.

In order for the mind of awakening to grow, you need to nurture it; you can't just sit idly by and wait for enlightenment to happen. The seed of awakened mind is already present in your very being, like a baby Buddha gestating inside you. But seeds and babies don't grow purely of their own volition – they need supportive conditions, like sunlight and water, or a mother's care, to inspire them and help them grow. Your mind, too, needs supportive conditions. There is so much momentum behind the speedy, forward-rushing, habitual patterns of ego. The engine on this particular freight train has a seemingly endless amount of fuel to burn, and it isn't about to stop on its own. To begin to slow down the train and eventually bring it to a halt, you need to start applying the brakes. And that takes some exertion.

"Exertion" is not a very exciting word. In fact, English

is often a poor language for conveying the meaning of ideas taught by the Buddha and written down in Pali and Sanskrit more than two thousand years ago. The English word "exertion" is serious, humorless, and rather unappealing. It makes you think of straining and sweating and "exerting" yourself to lift weights at the gym, or to study for a difficult exam, or to meet a crushing deadline at work.

In ancient Sanskrit texts, the word that is translated to English as "exertion" is *virya*. *Virya* is etymologically related to our English words "virile" and "vigor," implying a sense of strong effort or power. It's also related to the word "virtue," implying the application of this strong effort to the goal of awakening, for the benefit of yourself and everyone around you. But *virya* also means applying this effort with a light touch, with a sense of joy and humor that enlivens the spiritual path.

If you look at living examples of people who are very far along the path – accomplished masters of meditation and awakening – you don't see them slogging through their days looking weary and exhausted. Despite holding tremendous responsibilities, they're not resentful about how much the world expects of them or how little privacy or "me time" they have left at the end of the day. On the contrary, they radiate cheerfulness and joy and relaxation in everything they do, even in the midst of difficult circumstances. The paradoxical balance they strike is captured in a pith meditation instruction from the 12th-century Tibetan yogini Machik Labdron: "Alert! Alert! Yet, relax! Relax!"

Almost all of the Tibetan teachers I've studied with are known for their frequent laughter, playfulness, and child-like joy. They are always looking for ways to make students drop their serious trips and adopt a more light-hearted approach. When you spend time with a realized meditation master, they somehow always manage to pull the rug out from under you – maybe figuratively, or maybe literally.

It's part of their job description as a teacher. Some of the most direct and personal teachings I've received were meant to puncture the bubble of excessive self-seriousness in which I was floating. They were meant to get me to stop, recognize the absurdity of my own habitual patterns, drop it, smile, relax, and laugh at myself.

The 14th-century Tibetan teacher Longchenpa said, "Since everything is but an illusion, perfect in being what it is, having nothing to do with good or bad, acceptance or rejection, one might as well burst out laughing!"

Laughter is medicine for the heart, mind and body. It lowers blood pressure, dispels self-pity and depression, triggers neurochemical reactions that increase feelings of well-being, and strengthens your positive feelings of connection to others. It creates a sense of openness and space that wasn't there before, and an open mind leads to new possibilities.

Taking yourself very seriously, on the other hand, is usually a recipe for unhappiness. The more you invest your attention in all your personal dramas and your inflated sense of self-importance – the storm that rotates around the illusory center of I, I, I, me, me, me, mine, mine, mine – the more miserable and isolated you become. It's an ancient habit, a dysfunctional skill set that you've been honing since before you were born. But when you drop the excessively serious trance of selfing, even for a moment, you open your mind to the possibility of spontaneous joy. In doing so, you reconnect with your deeper nature and shed some of the baggage of the small, tragic self.

It's easy to get locked into a heavy sense of how solid and stuck and oppressive things are – whether it's outer circumstances or the apparent solidity of your own thoughts and habitual patterns, your seeming inability to change. But when you bring in a feeling of lightness and joy, a sense of the workability of everything, it can shift your experience. You can relax right in the midst of chaos, in the midst of exertion, instead of feeling like you have to achieve enlightenment and solve all the world's problems before relaxation will be possible. Stay the course and apply yourself with some effort to the path of awakening, but do it with a joyful heart and a relaxed mind.

The 8th-century Indian saint Shantideva described *virya* as sense of delight or joy in practicing virtue. He called it "joyful exertion." When you understand at a deep and personal level what leads to happiness and what leads to suffering, then you are like a patient who eagerly and happily takes the medicine that will cure his illness, even if that medicine tastes bitter at first. Once you know the instructions for waking up, you become eager to put them into practice, even if putting them into practice means giving up ego's familiar ground and going against your own deeply ingrained habitual patterns.

Shantideva also described the obstacle within us that so often prevents us from practicing *virya* or joyful exertion: laziness. He spoke about several common and habitual forms of laziness.

The first kind is just *plain old laziness* – an excessive attachment to comfort and pleasure and torpor and sleep. This is the sluggish laziness of not wanting to exert yourself because it's easier and less challenging to do nothing. The antidote to this first kind of laziness is to contemplate the Second Reminder, the truth of impermanence. When you remember the inevitability of death and the uncertainty of its timing, how short and vulnerable your lifespan really is, then you are reminded that you don't have time to waste. Awareness of death and impermanence helps you remember the urgency of the situation and overcome your laziness.

You have the opportunity right now to look within and work directly with your mind, to cultivate insight into the nature of reality, to transform your thoughts and emotions into fuel for awakening. This offer is available for a limited time only; it will not last. If you are not actually going inside and working with the raw stuff of your mind, then no matter how much spiritual practice you do, it's pointless.

You could circumambulate sacred sites and do prostrations and offer prayers; you could ring temple bells and offer candles and incense, dress up in robes and perform elaborate rituals; you could raise kundalini and get in touch with your chakras; you could sit rigidly in meditation for weeks on end. But without doing the real inside work necessary to transform your mind, all of this "spiritual" activity – no matter how diligent and virtuous it may look from the outside – is just more laziness and escapism. The real work lies in transforming your habitual patterns of greed, ignorance and aggression and your ingrained self-centeredness into openness, kindness, compassion, and peace. It's spiritual alchemy.

The second kind of laziness Shantideva described is being *despondent* or hopeless about yourself and your own ability to wake up. It's not uncommon to lose heart sometimes. You might feel that you are not even capable of meeting the circumstances of your life, much less of doing the hard work of transforming your habitual patterns of ego. Shantideva called this state of mind "mournful weariness." To combat it, he advised pulling yourself up by the bootstraps.

Whatever circumstance you are in, you can invoke a basic, unconditional sort of confidence in yourself and in the workability of the situation, even when things seem truly dire. Read Viktor Frankl's book *Man's Search for Meaning* and his descriptions of how he coped with life in the Nazi concentration camps. Somehow, he found it possible even in those unimaginably cruel and horrific circumstances to maintain a buoyancy of spirit, a resilience of the heart that helped him and some others survive.

This is not the arrogance of thinking that you will master every situation, or that things will always work out in your favor. It's simply the confidence that you have the innate wisdom to meet whatever arises with openness and compassion rather than shutting down. And even when you *do* shut down, you can meet your own shut down-ness with openness and compassion too. You can take responsibility for your own actions and state of mind, and stop placing all the blame on circumstances and other people. You can trust in yourself and your own awakened nature, even when you can't trust the people around you.

Friendliness toward yourself is part of the soft underbelly of *virya*, the feeling of joyful exertion. If you find yourself practicing in a way that feels uptight, like punishment or drudgery, then you're not being a very good friend to yourself. If you practice generosity, for example, but grumble to yourself about what an ungrateful jerk the person receiving your generosity is, then maybe there's something off with your internal attitude. Take a step back, take a breath of fresh air, and try to bring a little tenderness and light-hearted-ness into the situation. You can also laugh at yourself and your habitual patterns, rather than taking it all too seriously. Laugh at yourself joyfully, the way you would laugh with an old friend recalling stories of how silly you were in your younger days.

Shantideva's third kind of laziness is *self-contempt*, which is a lot like the despondency described above but sharper, more existential. When you fall into self-contempt, you feel that nothing matters; it's not even worth trying. You can't be bothered. It's a "Frankly, my dear, I don't give a damn" attitude, a couldn't-care-less approach to life. This attitude of contempt is ultimately just another form of laziness, another way of keeping yourself asleep in the cocoon of self-centered concerns. The world around you might be on fire, and you yourself might be burning up with rage or jealousy or addiction, but you just can't bring yourself to care. To hell with it all.

Last but not least, we have our favorite modern form of laziness: extreme busy-ness. Shantideva didn't actually talk about this one. That's because extreme busy-ness was probably not an endemic problem in 8th-century Indian societies. Shantideva could not have foreseen how extreme busy-ness would become many people's default mode in today's hyper-stimulated, hyper-connected society.

Always staying busy and distracted might seem like the opposite of laziness, because it involves so much activity and stimulation. But in fact it's just another way to keep yourself in the trance, sleepwalking through your days.

Think about it: If you are like most people living in any modern city, you probably plan and schedule every minute of your day and sometimes commit yourself to be in two or three places at once. Your carry your smartphone everywhere you go, so you can be constantly in touch with a ceaseless stream of news, communication, games, tweets, status updates, and entertainment choices. Perhaps you check your email and your text messages a hundred times a day, without even noticing the frequency. You might log on to social networks to tell your thousands of "friends" exactly where you are at the moment and what you're eating for lunch, or to provide your insights on the latest scandal surrounding whatever pop star everyone happens to be chattering about at the moment.

In the window of a coffee shop, you glimpse a college student with his papers and books on the table in front of him, simultaneously studying, listening to music on his headphones, watching a video on his laptop, and pecking out a text message on his mobile phone. We live in a society where 'multitasking' is not only accepted, but expected. We are encouraged to do three, five, or ten things simultaneously, at all times. It has become increasingly rare and strange to give our full attention to any one thing.

Who has time to do just one thing? That one thing is competing with several ongoing projects, five unread text messages, 14 emails that need a response, a 24-hour news cycle that cries out for your attention, and a stream of social media updates that have no importance whatsoever until the moment you look at them – then they suddenly require your sustained attention. You end up feeling like Gulliver among the tiny inhabitants of the island of Lilliput. Gulliver could not be captured by any one of the tiny people working alone, but he was captured while he slept and tied to the ground by the collective assault of hundreds of tiny people working together with their tiny ropes. No single email or text or project has total dominance over you, but collectively they overwhelm your mind and tie you to the ground, just like Gulliver. You are the prisoner of a thousand small demands upon your attention.

Meditation is the antidote to our modern addiction to busy-ness, speed and distraction. Through the practice of sitting still and doing nothing but resting your attention on the breath or some other simple object, you can train in unplugging from the hyperactive blur of information and stimuli. In meditation you counteract the laziness of always being busy, always leaning into the next moment, and you train in simply being present with your life as it is, in *this* moment. This is one of the greatest forms of compassion and kindness that you can practice towards yourself.

Knowing When to Let Go

Shantideva spoke about several qualities that support us in the practice of joyful exertion. One of these qualities is *moksha*, a Sanskrit word for liberation or freedom, but also for releasing, letting go, or sacrificing something.

Moksha could mean knowing when it's time to set your work aside and rest, so that you can continue later on in better form, without burning yourself out. Knowing your limits, when to say no, and when you need to take a break or just step back and breathe, are all necessary aspects of applying yourself with wisdom to the path of awakening and benefiting others. Running yourself into the ground – even if you do it with a noble intention – is not being friendly, gentle or compassionate towards yourself. When you burn out, you won't be the only one to suffer; you'll then be less capable of extending yourself to others, so they'll suffer too.

Moksha could also mean taking what you understand to be the right action in a given situation, then letting go of the outcome. So often we play god and try to control the results, forgetting that every situation unfolds within a complex and interdependent grid of causes and conditions that are beyond our ability to fully see, much less control. Often the best you can do is to take the right action, knowing that the result is out of your hands, and wait to see what kind of feedback comes to you from the world.

Letting go also means knowing when it's time to leave, when remaining in a given situation *at all* is simply not beneficial. Sometimes conditions, or human relationships, cross over a line from which there is no return. Nothing good is going to come of trying to keep working with it, and the best that can be done at that point is to walk away or ask the other person to leave. If you are in an abusive relationship, or if someone is stealing from you and manipulating you, then sometimes the best thing to do is to end the relationship altogether. Practicing love, tolerance, compassion, forgiveness and so on does not require making yourself into a doormat for other people's abuse.

Spirituality is not navel-gazing, or fiddling while Rome burns – it's being fully engaged in your life, your world and your relationships, with no separation and no prefabricated rules. As you grow on the path, you gain confidence that you can act when action is required, but your action comes from a different motivation than before. You don't have to 'fight back' in predictable ways, ruled by your own aggression and fear. Rather, your actions – even when you are fighting against an injustice – can come from a place of compassion and staying open to the possibility of other people's basic goodness (even when they're behaving atrociously).

Sometimes *moksha* means retreating from the situation and giving it space, before coming back to try again. Sometimes it means sitting down and having a frank conversation, and sharing your perspective in order to clear the air and let go of unspoken tensions. Sometimes it means protesting an injustice that harms other people. Sometimes it means giving someone a gift to show that you care. Sometimes it means calling the police and pressing charges against someone. Sometimes it means walking away entirely, and never looking back.

You get the picture. There is no one-size-fits-all solution, no predetermined course of action. The path is to meet every situation that arises with fresh awareness and an open heart, respond in whatever way is most beneficial, and then let go of trying to control the outcome.

Always Maintain a Joyful Mind

There's a famous Tibetan Buddhist slogan: "Always maintain only a joyful mind." This slogan is a strong counterpoint to 'mournful weariness' and to habitual patterns of criticizing and complaining. At first blush, it might sound naïve, or impossible. "Always maintain only a joyful mind? You've got to be kidding! Why would you even want to do that? You can't go around being joyful all the time. You need to be tough and skeptical, even a little bit pessimistic, to make it in this modern world." Right?

There is no situation that cannot be made better by infusing it with joy. Not a holiday greeting card sort of joy, which is superficial, plastic cheerfulness that can mask a denial of very real and very difficult situations, negativity and suffering in our lives. We're talking about unconditional joy, which clearly acknowledges reality but sees all situations as fundamentally workable – the kind of joyful resilience that burned within the heart of Viktor Frankl in the concentration camps, something he refused to allow the Nazis to take from him. With joyful exertion, every-

THE FOUR REMINDERS

thing is fuel for spiritual awakening.

Often, the difficult circumstances you encounter in life land in your lap with a great thud, with no prior warning. You didn't ask for your lover to leave you, or for your children to rebel against you, or for the stock you own to crash, or for the doctor to give you the diagnosis you didn't want to hear. But there it is; you have no choice in the matter. The question is: how do you react? How do you work with it? How do you hold your mind in response to what life throws at you?

Your spiritual practice, too, can be a practice of maintaining a joyful mind. How often do you sit down to meditate like you were going under the surgeon's knife, as if meditation were an unpleasant chore on your To-Do List, just one more thing that must be accomplished? With such an attitude, it's little wonder if you lack enthusiasm for practice.

When you find yourself getting too serious and heavy about your practice, turn the flame on the stove down a bit and let the pot simmer at a slower pace rather than boiling over. The challenge is often in knowing and respecting your own limits, and working at the level where you can maintain joy and enthusiasm.

You may think that your biggest obstacles and enemies are on the outside, in the form of people and circumstances that challenge you. You might get very worked up thinking about someone in your personal life who frustrates or angers you, or about the corrupt politicians you see in the news, or about the greedy financial speculators who caused the economy to crash, or about the corporations that decimate the environment in the name of profit, or about the war hawks who keep the world mired in violence and bloodshed.

You might point the finger of blame at those people for many of the issues you experience in your life and the problems you see in the world today. Those are all very real problems, in need of real solutions; and those people may, indeed, be responsible for creating and perpetuating many of these external problems.

But what hinders you on the path of your spiritual awakening isn't the people who irritate you or make you angry. It isn't the politicians or the corporations or the war hawks, or any other external figure – no matter how corrupt or misguided or galling they might be. In fact, no one other than you really has the power to prevent your awakening, because awakening is an inside job. Remember?

What hinders your awakening is your own reactive conditioning: your mournful weariness, your laziness, your arrogance, your contempt, your despair, your greed, your pride and your aggression – all the internal enemies that deprive you of joyful exertion and make you withdraw fearfully into your protective shell.

Chances are, you don't have much trouble exerting yourself whole-heartedly and enthusiastically in pursuit of external things that promise to make you comfortable and happy: money, possessions, relationships, careers, hobbies and so on. You display no shortage of joyful exertion when it comes to chasing after shiny objects and emotional peak experiences. Yet you may find it harder to pursue the only true and enduring form of well-being – spiritual awakening itself – with the same zeal and enthusiasm.

Awakening is not some distant goal to be achieved in the future, but something to be practiced in every moment. When you remember this, mournful weariness evaporates and your priorities become clear. Practicing joyful exertion, even in the midst of challenging circumstances, is like having a cool, refreshing breeze at your back – it makes the going a little bit easier. When you can work even with your own mistakes and obscurations – and those of others – with a touch of lightness and joy, then it's like a cool breeze enlivens all your actions and makes every situation you encounter more workable, spacious and relaxed. Doesn't that sound like a better way to go about your life?

THE FOUR REMINDERS

The Fourth Reminder calls on you to stop going in pointless circles chasing fulfillment in external things, and to recognize that true freedom and contentment comes from inside. Turning within to discover and nurture that freedom and contentment is not necessarily easy; it means swimming against a strong current of habits that has been flowing for a whole lifetime, perhaps longer. Swimming against the stream does take some effort; it doesn't just happen on its own. But how you experience that effort and that journey is somewhat up to you.

Which one sounds more appealing? Joyful exertion? Or mournful weariness? You choose.

CONTEMPLATING THE FOURTH REMINDER

Contemplation: Assessing Your Priorities

After contemplating the first three reminders, you appreciate the incredible opportunity you have for waking up in this life; you know that time is truly running out and that this life will be over in a flash; and you understand that every single thing you do matters and has consequences.

How can you apply the wisdom of these insights to your life? How much of your time do you want to spend pursuing temporary pleasures and peak experiences, and how much do you want to spend pursuing genuine freedom and awakening from within? What are your real values and priorities in life? Is the actual way you are living in alignment with those values and those priorities, or do you need to make some adjustments?

Contemplation: False Refuges

This contemplation is inspired by verses written several hundred years ago by two Buddhist teachers, Padampa

Sangye and the Ninth Karmapa. Spend time reflecting on each question, and ask yourself: to what extent are you looking for meaning and fulfillment in these things? Are they truly reliable refuges?

- *Homes, objects and wealth*: Material comforts are like clouds and mist, without any graspable substance. If you have these things, how long do you imagine they will last? If you don't have them, how much of your time and energy do you spend pursuing them?

    A few years ago, I visited friends who live in a beautiful house in Halifax, Nova Scotia. The house is built on the same spot where their previous home was destroyed in a freak wildfire that tore through the neighborhood quite suddenly, whipped up by winds blowing off the ocean. My friends lost their home and all of their possessions to the fire that day – they even lost the family dog. They were lucky to escape with their own lives as they fled the neighborhood. They told me that since the fire, they have never been able to relate in quite the same way to material things like homes and possessions. Although they rebuilt a lovely new home on the same spot as the previous one, the fire taught them, the hard way, that things like homes, materials objects, and wealth really are ephemeral, and they can vanish suddenly. Contemplate how everything that appears to "belong" to you could disappear in an instant. Who would you be without your things?

- *Popularity and fame*: Even in ancient times, human beings sought after popularity and fame. Renowned warriors and kings and queens gained power in society, and are still talked about today in history books. These days, with celebrity culture and the rampant narcissism fueled by social media, our obsession with popularity and fame has reached a new, frenetic crescendo. But for all the energy we invest in pursuing popularity and fame, they have about as much substance and staying power as an echo. Think about how many "stars" you've seen come and go in just the past five or ten years. How long does even the most popular and famous person stay in good favor with the public? Do you imagine that being more popular or more famous would bring you lasting satisfaction?

- *Food and drink*: Turn on any one of numerous cable TV channels today and you'll see 24-hour programming devoted to the cult of food and drink. Gourmet cooking shows, restaurant reviews, international food travel shows, elaborate chef competitions – all designed to showcase and celebrate our culinary obsession and its heroic figures. But even the most delicious, gourmet meal quickly turns to excrement after you eat it – and all excrement is the same. How much importance and meaning do you attach to culinary delights and pursuing your favorite foods?

- *The body*: Our society is obsessed with youth and physical beauty, and we invest enormous amounts of money, time and energy into maintaining the body's appearance. But the human body is a sack of blood, pus and meat, held up on a rickety frame of bony sticks. It will soon be a corpse, and afterwards it will rot in the earth or be burned to ashes in an oven. How much importance do you attach to your body, to the way it looks and feels, to pampering it and worrying about how it's perceived by other people? How much help will your body be to you when death comes to take it? Of course you should guard your health and care for your body; it's a precious gift that sustains you and helps you in this lifetime. But where does concern for your body cross the line into obsession?

- *Friends and family*: All of your friends and family members are impermanent. One by one, death takes them from you; or, through betrayal or conflict, they can suddenly transform from loved ones into hated enemies or rivals. People can also drift away from you, becoming so distant that you lose your bond to them. Even the most passionate love affairs and marriages sometimes end in bitter divorce, and occasionally even murder. Do you rely excessively on friends and family, imagining they will always be there for you?

- *Careers*: The realm of jobs and commerce is as shifting and unstable as the wind. Even if you're very successful at what you do, you might suddenly lose it all. You could be replaced in your job by someone younger who will work for less money. Or your whole company could go bankrupt. I was once laid off from a full-time job with only two weeks' notice, and no severance package. My bosses loved me and didn't want to let me go, but they had no choice because the company had hit a financial roadblock and had to lay off half their full-time staff in a single stroke. Think of the once giant, sprawling companies that collapsed and vanished during the most recent economic recession, not to mention the countless small businesses that disappear each day and never make the news. Do you seek your life's meaning in your career or job? Are you driven by ambition to pour yourself into your work? How much help do you imagine your career or job will provide to you at the moment of death?

Contemplation: Renouncing the Causes of Suffering
Contemplate examples from your life when you have caused trouble for yourself or others through your own actions or attitudes of clinging or aversion. Can you think of times when you acted aggressively towards someone

else, or when you behaved selfishly and without consideration for someone else, or when you were overly attached, clingy, or addicted? How did this make you feel?

Reflect on the unnecessary suffering you caused for yourself and for others, and cultivate a sense of revulsion towards the actions that caused this suffering. How might the outcome have been different if you had acted, instead, from openness, compassion and kindness?

Now look at the present moment in your life. Are there situations where you could apply those qualities in order to create a better future for yourself and those around you?

Contemplation: What's Your Realm?

Read over the descriptions of the six realms of existence described by the Buddha, in the chapters on the First and Fourth Reminders. Which realm sounds most like you? Is there a particular realm or psychological state in which you commonly get trapped? Has this changed over time? Looking back 10 years ago, or 20 years ago, did you inhabit the same realm then as you do now?

Look at the people closest to you and make a guess about which realm they inhabit most, in their minds. Is it the same as yours, or different? Imagining yourself in their shoes for a moment, how does their experience of the world differ from yours? Why?

•••••••

For additional suggestions on contemplating the Fourth Reminder, refer to the accompanying Study and Discussion Guide, which you can download at:

www.thefourreminders.com

AFTERWORD

The spiritual path has its stages, like any other journey. It's like climbing a mountain: you see things differently depending on how far up the mountain you are.

When you first start climbing that mountain, your view of what you're doing – and why you're doing it – is rather limited, like pictures taken through a narrow lens that captures only part of the view. You are primarily concerned with your own quest for personal awakening and freedom from suffering. The Four Reminders help at this stage of the path because they turn the mind towards the goal of putting an end to suffering, as described by the Buddha in his earliest teachings. They remind you, as you stand on the mountain's lower third, that the climb is not going to be easy; it's going to require a lot of energy and effort; and you'd better be serious about it, and well prepared for it, before you start climbing.

The Four Reminders focus on the inner work of seeing through your own illusions and sharpening your personal commitment to seeking the truth. The first step in waking up is to let go of the dream world you lived in as you slept; you can't hope to be very awake, or to be of much help to others, if you are still in the spell of delusion, grasping at comfort and security in false refuges. The Four Reminders strip away four of the veils that habitually dim and distort your own vision of reality and hinder your capacity to be fully awake in the midst of your life. They turn your mind in the direction of awakening.

Once your mind is turned in that direction, then a different picture starts to come into focus. You swap the narrow lens for a wide-angle lens that offers a broader view. You see that your own liberation cannot really be separated from your relationships to other sentient beings. We are all in this together, and together we suffer and find liberation from suffering.

This reflects something that most spiritual traditions seem to have in common. Almost without exception, they emphasize altruism: the importance of realizing our interdependence with others and acting out of concern for others' well-being and spiritual care. This is why spiritually mature beings downplay self-centered concerns and emphasize the welfare of others. In such people, the childish ego's "What about me?" attitude has been supplanted entirely by a compassionate concern for others' happiness and well-being. Take any great spiritual leader – the Buddha, Jesus, the Dalai Lama, Mother Teresa, Gandhi, Martin Luther King, Jr. – and think about what they all have in common. They all devoted themselves single-pointedly and fearlessly to the path of altruism and compassion, with little residual trace of a self-seeking ego.

As your view broadens, your motivation for being on the spiritual path also starts to change. It becomes less about helping yourself and relieving your own suffering, and more about helping others and relieving their suffering too. This spirit of self-sacrificing love and compassion for others is what lies behind the symbolic crucifixion of Jesus Christ, his redemptive sacrifice for all of humanity. It is behind the principle of *Tikkun Olam*, the idea from Kabbalah (Jewish mysticism) of doing good deeds in order to 'heal the universe,' thereby returning the Holy Spark that is each sentient being to the divine source from which it sprang. It is the reason why some addicts and alcoholics in 12-Step programs stick around in the program long after they've essentially overcome the addictions that brought them there: because they find new meaning and purpose in giving back and helping others discover the same freedom they have found. It is the vision behind the Buddhist archetype of the Bodhisattva, the noble being who works tirelessly for the benefit of others and strives towards enlightenment so that everyone may also reach that state.

As you move into this second stage of the spiritual journey, a much larger view comes into focus: you realize that you are traveling the path not just for yourself and your own benefit, but for the benefit of all beings. Recognizing our fundamental interconnectedness and the fact that we need each other to do the work of waking up, you put compassion and loving-kindness front and center. Helping others wake up becomes your main goal, an end in itself, and your own awakening is a means to achieving that end: when you, yourself, wake up, then you will better understand how to help others wake up.

In a way, this turns your world, and your personal project of awakening for your own benefit, upside-down. Making the commitment to put others first and focus on helping them requires an unflinching allegiance to growing up and leaving behind the childish ego's petty concerns.

A word that pops up often in the Buddha's teachings about this second stage of the path is 'emptiness.' Emptiness describes how you experience the world once you move beyond your fixated ideas about who you are, who other people are, and what the situation is. It does not mean that the world is an empty vacuum or a void in which nothing exists and nothing happens. It means that nothing exists, and nothing happens, in the way you ordinarily *think* it does.

Ordinarily, you think that appearances are real and that things – objects, people, situations, perceptions, words, thoughts and feelings – truly are the way they appear to be. But the Buddha taught that nothing is what it appears to be at first. Everything that appears is like an echo or a mirage, a phantasmagoric glimmer of experience arising and passing away in mind's mirror. When you try to pin anything down, you find that it is empty; there isn't anything that you can grasp in your hands (or with your mind) and finally say, "This is real. This is solid and permanent. This is me. This is mine."

Whether or not it's to your ego's liking, everything is much more fluid than that. Cup your hands to lift a handful of water towards your face. Now try to grasp the water in your fist and see what happens.

Sacred World

In the third stage of the spiritual journey, as you ascend the very top of the mountain, the view is incomparable. The final vestiges of the illusory separations between self and other, between self and world, between "you" and "your life," start to fall away, and everything you see is revealed as sacred. Inspired by unconditional confidence in the basic goodness of your own mind, you regard every aspect of your life, every being you meet, and every experience that arises as the path of awakening. Basic goodness means that your inherent potential for awakening – your Buddha nature – does not depend on any external conditions. It doesn't depend on things going your way, or on you being comfortable in a world that caters to your preferences. This awakened potential is simply the nature of the mind itself, present in every moment of experience.

On the Buddhist path, the most "advanced" meditation practices involve looking directly at the awakened nature of mind in each moment, resting in naked awareness, and letting go of any attempts to change, control or improve it. The idea that liberation is to be sought and attained in some theoretical future moment, in some other kind of

THE FOUR REMINDERS

experience than what you are having in the present moment, is fundamentally mistaken. Seeing the freshness of whatever arises here and now, and resting in the vivid, awakened quality of mind in each moment, *is* the essence of realization. This includes the glitter and the garbage, the lotus flower and the mud in which it grows, the gourmet food and the excrement it is destined to become in a few hours.

This view entails a radical re-interpretation of the spiritual path because there is nothing that stands outside of it. Every aspect of the world you experience – what you see and hear and feel, what you say and do and think – is all the play and expression of inherently awakened mind, and it's all sacred. Everything that appears –whether you label it as good or bad, pleasant or unpleasant – is equal in being a window into the awakened state of mind. Nothing can be an obstacle to awakening when everything is regarded as the path of awakening.

In fact, the things you ordinarily think of as the biggest obstacles to awakening are actually powerful catalysts for awakening. Even your ugliest emotional hang-ups and your most painful breakdowns can be fuel for awakening if you are able to experience them with total acceptance, openness and awareness.

At earlier stages of the path, emotional afflictions – lust, anger, jealousy, pride, and so on – are seen as enemies or obstacles to awakening. These emotional storms are regarded as the causes of suffering, and the goal of spiritual practice in the early stages is to quiet the storm's energy and gain peace-of-mind. You turn away from the storm or apply some kind of remedy or opposing force within your mind in order to pacify it. But at this third stage of the path, the approach is altogether different. Rather than steering clear of emotional storms or trying to pacify them, the fearless practitioner who sees everything as sacred welcomes the storm's energy and goes directly into it. You can regard even the most gnarly attack of anger, jealousy or lust as the vivid experience of mind's empty yet awakened nature. In fact, the more intense the experience, the more vividly it can reveal mind's nature.

Try to rest directly in that energy without acting out on it and without applying labels or concepts to it – without trying to categorize it as good or bad, without trying to stop it, amp it up, or manipulate it in any way. Simply see it and experience its energy, with full awareness; there is nothing more that needs to be done. Thoughts and emotions self-liberate when you no longer fixate on them.

When the very energies that move through your mind lose their power to hook you and pull you back into the trance, then you begin to taste true freedom. No longer on autopilot and sleepwalking through your life, you are not so easily trapped in old habitual patterns and ways of reacting to your experience. You can move through life with eyes wide open, fundamentally awake and open to the world's suffering and beauty, its wretchedness and glory.

Your human life is a precious opportunity to discover this freedom and awakening for yourself; that would be the most meaningful thing you could do. But this life has an expiration date, and it's coming up soon; there's no time to waste. Everything you do, say, and think creates ripples; every action has a corresponding reaction, moving you closer to freedom or further away from it. And for heaven's sake, haven't you spent enough time and energy going in circles? You know where that has gotten you.

Your whole life, you've been hearing an alarm clock going off in your heart and mind, but you kept hitting the snooze button and lapsing back into dreams.

Your time for living in the trance, dreaming away your nights and sleepwalking through your days, is over. You're too aware; you know too much now to keep going in that direction. The Four Reminders have opened your eyes and pointed you in the direction of awakening. Now it's up to you to keep going. Don't go back to sleep.

It's time to wake up. For real.

ADDITIONAL RESOURCES

Official Web Site:
www.TheFourReminders.com
Visit the Web site to download a variety of resources, listen to guided meditations, and join the mailing list to get news about *The Four Reminders* and related content from the author.

Study and Discussion Guide
At the Web site, you can download a free Study and Discussion Guide with questions and suggestions for working with The Four Reminders. This guide is useful for either individual contemplation or group study in a book club or practice group.

The Study and Discussion Guide offers suggestions for taking your contemplation of the Four Reminders further, with recommendations for additional readings, related films, song selections that reinforce the themes touched upon in the book, and more.

ADDITIONAL RESOURCES

Social Images

On the Web site, you can also view and collect many premade images with pithy messages from *The Four Reminders*. Designed for sharing on Instagram, Facebook, Pinterest, Twitter, and other social media, these images are a fun way to contemplate and share the teachings. Simply click to share your favorite images with friends, or download them all to create your own library of Four Reminders-themed digital cards for daily contemplation.

ABOUT THE AUTHOR

Dennis Hunter has been teaching and writing about meditation and Buddhist philosophy since 2002. He began his practice in the Shambhala Buddhist tradition, and later studied closely with Dzogchen Ponlop and Pema Chödrön. He lived for two years as a Buddhist monk at Pema Chödrön's monastery in Nova Scotia, where he wrote much of the material in *The Four Reminders*.

He is author of the book *You Are Buddha: A Guide to Becoming What You Are*. His blog One Human Journey has been active for nearly a decade, with hundreds of articles and resources. He is also a contributing writer for HuffPost. His guided audio meditations can be found on the Insight Timer meditation app.

Dennis lives in Miami Beach with his husband, the yoga teacher Adrian Molina; they co-founded the Warrior Flow school of yoga, and together they lead classes, workshops, and international yoga and meditation retreats.

PRAISE FOR *THE FOUR REMINDERS*

"In The Four Reminders, Dennis Hunter offers a classic body of Tibetan Buddhist teachings and meditations on the proverbial facts of life using a refreshing and articulate voice. With a great gift for updating the language and context of these invaluable lessons from the ancient world, Hunter reminds us that Buddhist wisdom was never meant to be mystical or exotic. Instead, these pages give you something much more important: practical advice for being human." — **Ethan Nichtern**, bestselling author of *The Road Home*

"Reading *The Four Reminders* gave me the unique experience of something that few books can claim: being guided into a contemplation on what is most essential to know (and embody) if one is to live fully and freely. Hunter has woven a profound journey, rendering key and authentic Buddhist wisdom in a way that anyone can understand and apply. It is an invitation to all and any one of us, not just those already walking the spiritual path, to courageously embrace the eternal truths that lead to lasting happiness and peace." — **Yogarupa Rod Stryker**, founder of ParaYoga and author of *The Four Desires: Creating a Life of Purpose, Happiness, Prosperity, and Freedom*

"The Four Reminders is a welcome addition to practicing what matters most. This book personally guides us through the practice so that we can reflect on our thoughts, words, and actions. May it serve to free all beings from living in fear." — **Sensei Koshin Paley Ellison**, cofounder of New York Zen Center for Contemplative Care and editor of *Awake at the Bedside: Contemplative Teachings on Palliative and End of Life Care*

"This book presents the transformational teachings of Buddhist mindfulness in a powerful and provocative way. Hunter doesn't shy away from challenging the reader to address deep-seated personal and cultural assumptions on the road to happiness and freedom. By grounding his insights in the ancient spiritual tradition of Buddhism, Hunter offers more than the average self-help happiness book. His years of discipline and devotion to a personal spiritual practice give his insights a level of weight and groundedness often missing from similar books. I highly recommend this book to anyone seeking a key to unlock the path to peace in their lives." — **Kino MacGregor**, bestselling author, international yoga teacher, and co-founder of OmStars

"A candid, nuanced, and often playful invitation to explore the Four Reminders. May this insightful and accessible book help many people find meaning and freedom in life. I rejoice that this book is available to open the door to these teachings." — **Gelong Loden Nyima**

"'The reason karma is so infallible,' Hunter insightfully reminds his readers, 'is because there's no way to escape or hide from your own mind.' Rather, a healthy emphasis should be placed on improving karma by enhancing the mind, and this lucid book is full of hard-won and well-phrased pointers on how even the most stressed-out readers can start to bring that about in their own lives. A smart, eminently readable Buddhist guide to achieving an inner awakening." — **Kirkus Reviews**

Printed in Great Britain
by Amazon